About Student Government Solutions:

Student Government Solutions is focused on giving college and university student governments the resources and training they need to be successful. The goal is to help build outstanding student leaders through providing high quality training materials, workshops and instruction, as well as project/issue specific aid for student governments all across the country.

About the Author:

Eric Williams attended the University of California, Irvine where he studied Political Science, Economics and Management. In college Eric served as the Vice President of Administrative Affairs in the Associated Students of UC Irvine. During his time in student government Eric helped establish UC Irvine's first free legal clinic and a mentorship program aimed at boosting commuter student involvement on campus. He also served as a leader in the California Public Interest Group where he organized many media events and student mobilization campaigns.

Written by Eric Williams

Acknowledgements and Legal Information

Thanks to the following people for their support:
Lindsay, Nick, Lilan, Beth Krom, Liz and my parents

Table of Contents

Introduction

You want to learn something new; and you need it quick. You've just joined student government for the first time, you have no idea what you're doing yet and you're looking for a place to start. Or you may have been in student government for years and you're feeling like you could use a few more skills to really make your new project take off. Maybe you've been hung up on one issue for months, you want to get things off the ground and you're looking to this book for a little inspiration. *The Essential Student Government Guide* is just what you need to make your projects successful like never before and reach a new level of effectiveness you never thought possible. This manual won't have a solution to everything you'll run into, but with a little creativity you'll be able to make these time tested strategies work for you.

For over 100 years students in Student Government Associations have been at the forefront for leadership and change at colleges and universities all across the county. You are no exception to this tradition. Your responsibility in student government is to serve the student body. You will be making important decisions on behalf of your fellow students by promoting quality programs and policies to make their time at college more successful and enjoyable. This guide will cover all the basic skills you'll need to be successful in student government and help you achieve the goals you've been chosen to accomplish.

Use this guide as a resource for setting and accomplishing your goals. The best way to start is to review each part of this guide and then focus in on what you specifically need. There are many fictional examples to help you understand the major concepts. Many of the strategies and tools in this manual you have never considered using before, but can be very beneficial. These new and exciting ideas will help launch your project into success. It's important to know what skills are available in this book so that you can learn how to use those tools as you need them. The more you know the more you'll be able to bring to your project, whether it is putting on the most amazing concert your school has ever seen or advocating for your campus to put solar panels on new buildings.

Chapter 1: Now That You're in Student Government

You have the power to make amazing changes to your campus and to the lives of your fellow students. To take action to accomplish your goals, you need to think about where to start, what you want to work on and what your position entails. This will be the first step in determining what more you can learn and what you can do with your position.

What Kind of Student Leader Do You Want to be?

Do you enjoy being in charge of what is going on? Were you always chosen to be a leader of groups you were involved in? Do you want to try to have a positive impact on your campus? Are you drawn to the power and influence the government system provides? Did you join because you want to fix a broken system?

Each person brings vital experience and a unique point of view to student government based on their own interests and priorities. What do you want to accomplish during your time in student government? The key is to understand what your strengths and objectives so that you can set a plan in motion to get it done. Later we will help identify your core issues and what will make you achieve success by using the tools in this manual.

Helpful Questions to ask yourself:

1. What do I care about?
2. What are the top 3 issues that I feel are facing my fellow students?
3. What are my unique skills?
4. How can my unique skills benefit my fellow students?

Why does the Student Government Exist?

Student government exist to provide governance and advocacy on behalf of the student body and to benefit the students it serves. Governing involves making decisions and implementing policies that affect the student body, and working with campus administrators to ensure responsible decision making on behalf of the student body. Student leaders must also work to ensure that students' rights are upheld and that policies and programs are established that benefit the student body. Student government is far more complicated than most people think, which is why you should invest the time to learn as much as possible about your own system.

Every student government has some type of constitution and corresponding documents that articulate the ideals of the organization and the responsibilities of the members of that body. When students at your campus first created your student government they established the purpose for the organization and objectives for it to accomplish. Governing bodies evolve over time as the responsibilities and purview adapt to a changing environment. Request the documents that are the foundation for the organization and review them to get a good idea about the reason your student government exists and what it's guiding principals are. They will provide a roadmap to steer you through your time in student government.

Your Role as Part of the Team
Elected Officials:

Official duties and responsibilities vary from position to position and from school to school, but one definition encompasses all of them. You were elected to represent your fellow students and advocate on their behalf. This could mean you have an office of campaign directors working to solve problems with student housing, food services, and transportation, casting votes on important policy decisions that affect the way student funds are spent, or even defending students' rights against invasive campus policies.

This position requires you to be a leader, a planner and a motivator more than anything else. In a very real way you are the face and the voice of students all over campus, and so it becomes your duty to seek out and identify problems students are having all across the school.

> Student government provides you a training ground to use your own experience to test new ideas about leadership and strategies for success in a relatively low stress and low consequence environment. Try something new and don't let the fear of failure keep you from achieving your goals.

Directors/Commissioners/Coordinators:

You have been hand-picked by the elected students to be a leader in achieving the goal of making student life better on campus. You may be responsible for planning and organizing a major fall festival, administrating a legal clinic for your fellow students, or attending academic board meetings. These projects rely on your energy and enthusiasm to make it work and get it done. You can inspire the interns and volunteers to accomplish the goals because you understand the details of the campaign or event. You have a great deal of responsibility serving in this role because the elected officer who appointed you doesn't have time to work on the details of your assignment and is relying on you to accomplish it instead.

Interns and Volunteers:

Interns and volunteers in student government make up the backbone of the organization, doing anything and everything that needs to get done. You have the opportunity to learn about many different aspects of student government and contribute your ideas and energy into ongoing projects. You can even start your own project. Interns and volunteers are given real responsibilities and are often relied upon to help direct the logistics of an event or make sure that everyone is going to be in attendance at an important meeting. These duties take some of the load off of the elected officials and directors with busy schedules. Interns and volunteers are in a great position to learn, grow, and become the next leaders in student government.

Advantages of being in Student Government

Students – Fellow student leaders are the single best resource that you have in student government. The success of many projects hinge on the quality of the individuals and teams working in it and how well they are able to motivate other students to take action. Event a highly motivated group of people with few resources is a force to be reckoned with.

Funding – Student governments have unequaled access to funding compared to other student activities. These funds have been granted by the student body in the form of a tax on tuition to provide the services and support that is part of student government. This funding goes to various initiatives each year aimed at making student life better.

Legitimacy – The people in student government are elected to represent the student body or chosen by those elected students. Student government is viewed as the official governmental body to make decisions and take action on behalf of the student body. This gives everyone in student government the ability to work with administrators and students with the official backing of the student body at large. Students working at all levels of student government to have a high level of access to campus administrators and community decision makers.

Dedicated staff – Many student governments have a few professional, non-student staff to handle accounting for the organization or manage various student government businesses and operations. This allows the student leaders to focus on pursuing a variety of initiatives to make the campus better rather than getting bogged down in administrative duties.

History – Student government is an evolving and growing organization, constantly building on its previous achievements. Use the already established relationships to help boost the success of your campaign. You can also learn from the mistakes that have been made in the past to avoid the pitfalls you will encounter in the future. In fact, many traditions exist in order to minimize problems that have come up in the past. Do some research about your organization so that you can avoid falling into the same problems that have been resolved in the past and build on previous successes.

Unique Responsibilities

- **Pass resolutions and policies** – Legislative bodies can make statements that represent the opinions of the students on your campus. Such a large number of people representing one view can go a long way to push an issue along or make legitimate policy decisions.

- **Establish groups of experts to solve problems** – You can bring together students and campus experts to work on generating a specific answer to a problem on your campus. For Example, you can establish a board to pursue environmental sustainability issues on campus and the possibility of using solar power.

- **Mobilize students into action** – Many students are interested in getting involved. All they need is leadership and organization by their elect student leaders to make positive change happen. Use various strategies discussed in this manual to get students involved like Tabling, Class Presentations and On-line Organizing.

- **Advocate for a cause** – As a representative of the student body it is your duty to ensure that students' opinions are heard on major issues within the campus administration and in the community.

- **Reach important decision makers** – Identify and communicate with local community leaders, elected officials, and school administrators about important student issues.

- **Outreach and Communications** – As the most connected and well informed students on campus, the responsibility falls on you to communicate important news to the student body. Examples: rate hikes for student loans, new judicial policies or any issue that directly affects them.

- **Establish programs** – Identify problems that students face on a regular or irregular basis and try to rectify that issue. An example could be establishing a free legal clinic to provide students with the occasional needed legal advice in a private and confidential setting.

Summary

Throughout this section we mainly focused on identifying and understanding your role in student government. With your new roles and responsibilities it is important to figure out what you want to accomplish and what drives you. The more you're able to understand about yourself and about the student government you are in, the more you'll be able to accomplish your goals. Keep in mind the unique abilities student government's provide and what they allow you to do because you can leverage them to maximize your outcome.

Chapter 2: Governing and Representing the Student Body

One of your major roles in student government is to serve as a team member, a leader and a decision maker on behalf of the student body. No matter your position you'll be asked to weigh in on decisions that directly affect students in one way or another. Decision making is not easy. Sometimes the choices can involve making tough decisions between what you view as a bad choice and a worse choice. The tools in this chapter will help make that job easier by identifying many of the problematic areas and giving you tips to resolve them.

Funding

Deciding how money should be used is one of the most highly debated topics you'll encounter year after year in student government. Because so many students inside and outside of student government have a stake in the distribution of funds, tempers will flare and debates will get heated. Everyone feels that their activities are important and should be fully funded, but there is never enough money to fully satisfy everyone and every valuable program.

Even funds set aside for your programs from the student government budget should be treated with care. You may have been delegated $2,000 to solve textbooks affordability issues, but if you can get away with using only $500, without sacrificing quality, you should try your best to do so. Someone else might end up needing that funding to make their program a success. Don't waste the money if you can avoid it. In the end, the students have many other expenses that they have to worry about including books, tuition and rent. It falls on you to make sure the money they are contributing to student government is being used in the best manner possible.

Money in student government is the students' money, not student government's!

Always remember that the money you get in order to fund any of your projects should never be used for unnecessary expenses.

Tips for Saving Money

1. **Pretend you don't have any**: How would you accomplish your goal with zero funding? You would be very surprised to find out how many things can be done with very few expenses if you really have to.

2. **Get donations from local businesses**: Local businesses are usually willing to contribute some amount of food or store resources to projects and events going on at a campus close by. Always remember to mention their contribution and thank them later!

3. **Reuse old materials**: Sometimes you don't use all of your supplies, posters or other materials from a past project. Design your posters with a fill-in-the-blank date box so you can reuse them for multiple events over the course of the year! You can also make use of equipment that is getting old or out of date by repurposing it for another project.

4. **Put in a little more time**: Frequently you can find a solution by not taking an easy way out, it just takes more effort. An example could be building relationships with you campus newspaper editors to get a student government statement put in the paper rather than buying expensive ad space.

Spending Money vs. Saving Time:

Sometimes you need to get a task done quickly and you just have to pay for it. The goal of planning is to limit how often you get caught off guard. Try to spend money in a methodical manner rather than in an emergency situation.

Resolving Funding Disputes

1. **Evaluate necessary vs. desired funding**: What funding is absolutely necessary for the success of the event and what funding would make it better?

2. **Contribution to the campus and community**: Does the program or activity add to the social, cultural or educational quality of the campus and community?

3. **Wide vs. narrow audience**: Will the event draw many people from all over the campus or is it simply going to attract those putting on the event?

4. **Direct benefit**: Which and how many students will this new program or event directly benefit?

5. **Fundraising activities**: Is the student government or club requesting money for an event or to raise money for a cause or for their own club? Note: Most student governments do not allow funds to be used in this way, but may have a temporary loan system for it.

6. **Political campaigns or religious services**: Typically student funds are not authorized to be used to support specific candidates or campaigns, but may be used by the student government for advocacy on behalf of the student body. A fine line also exists for programs that may be put on by a religious organization but not have a religious element.

The Image Factor

Earning the trust and confidence of the student body has an immeasurable value, allowing you and your programs to succeed, getting more students out to events, and bringing in the very best leaders for future generations. Creating a reputation of effectiveness and confidence on campus may seem like a purely superficial exercise, but it enhances the actual good work being done by your student government.

1. **Be Visible**: Put your logo on everything to let people know all the activities your student government is involved in. Most people don't realize the scope of programs and involvements student government's have. When they keep seeing your logo popping up on virtually everything that is well run, they'll have a positive impression of your organization.

2. **Be Effective**: Nothing gives people more confidence than seeing event after event go off without a major problem because of proper organization and thorough planning. Always take the time to plan and organize your projects on the front end to ensure you're not scrambling to get everything pulled together at the last minute. The quality will show. (See Chapter 7: Planning)

3. **Publicize Everything**: If you're having a lot of success with a particular issue, but nobody knows about what you're doing, people will still think you're slacking off. Send out a press release to the local media and campus newspaper for every new event and every time your project gains significant ground. The students will repeatedly see the victories you're winning for their benefit. (See Chapter 4: Getting the Word Out...)

4. **Include Everyone**: Conflicts and bad reputations in student government are caused by a lack of information and inclusion. Your opponent's fears will be lessened by talking through the problems and the number of factors that are involved. They may still disagree with you, but they'll respect you for listening to their concerns. At least they won't think you're incompetent. Do your best to create coalitions and build consensus to pursue the best course of action.

Getting Input from Students: Surveying and Communication

Your role in student government, whether elected, appointed, or hired is not to do everything the student body wants you to do, but to blend the opinions of the campus with your own sense of direction. Use your expertise to evaluate what the most beneficial decision for the student body would be and to weight all the factors involved.

However, making assumptions with the best of intentions can backfire, costing you time and effort on a project when it turns out students were not in support of. For that reason it's important to combine your intuition with backup information from surveys, forums, and personal contact to ensure your vision of reality is the same as everyone else's.

Issue Forums

Have students from around campus with knowledge of an issue you are facing or experience with events that you want to do get together for a brainstorming session. Getting everyone together in one place can be an excellent way to get feedback on your ideas and to come up with new ones. It's also great to bring in some students who don't have a vested interest in that particular issue to give critiques. Issue forums give students the sense that their student government cares what they think, and is willing to listen.

> **Getting it Done**: Send out a focused or campus wide e-mail announcing the forum date and time. Contact clubs that have an interest in the topic of the forum and get club members to commit to coming. Ask your friends or people you know in your student government if they know someone who is interested. Make sure you set an agenda for the meeting, confirm attendance, and are ready to lead the discussion. (See How to Run an Effective Meeting)

Surveys

Surveys allow you to get quantifiable answers to confirm or disprove your ideas. Surveys are essential for supporting your position when the costs of your proposal are high and when you're working with people in high level positions who have to weigh all the factors involved. Survey accuracy relies on having random respondents from a random set of backgrounds. This makes creating and administering an effective survey very difficult and very sensitive.

> **Getting it done**: Write a survey questionnaire after figuring out what information you need to collect. Follow the tips in this chapter for details about writing the survey. You can administer the survey through an on-line method such as random e-mail distribution, made easier if your campus has an already established system that allows students to write and conduct surveys using campus e-mail addresses. Another option is to conduct face to face surveys around campus. This option requires you to do the survey at different times of the day and week as well as different places on campus, so it is very labor intensive.

Watch out! Don't survey only your friends or group members. The survey needs to be taken by a random segment of the student population, or by a random arrangement of your target group. If not, you take the risk that your survey will be biased by a common opinion that may be shared by a small group.

Tips for writing an unbiased survey:

1. Keep the survey short: 5-10 questions.

2. Identify what information would be most valuable to collect. Frequently you need to ask a few indirect questions to get at a more accurate response.

3. Include only what you need to know. Avoid extraneous and unnecessary questions and put the most important questions first.

4. Keep question wording simple and understandable. Don't assume your respondents know an issue in detail.

5. Logically order your questions so that the flow makes sense and that the order of responses are not leading them to your own conclusion.

6. Avoid leading questions and titles that demand a specific response. You're asking what they think, not to confirm what you think.

7. Moderate survey options to account for a full range of answers from positive to negative

8. Specific choices work better than open-ended questions. You'll be able to quantify your results rather than having a general range of responses that you have to decipher.

Bad Survey Question: Do you think the Parking Department is bad because of its price gauging and ticketing tactics? (Circle one)

Possibly   Yes   Absolutely

Good Survey Question: Rate your impression of the campus Parking Department based upon your experience. (Circle one)

Negative   Indifferent   Positive   Don't Know Enough

Club Visits

When you're looking for general feedback and opinions visit clubs and organizations at your school. These students tend to be the most invested in the success of the campus and will have more to say about the issues student government is involved in. They'll be appreciative that you took the time to find out what they had to say. This can also be a great way to boost your student government's image on campus.

> **Getting it done**: Contact the department that has records of clubs and organizations on your campus and get a list of club leaders. Then contact the club and schedule a time to go to their meeting. Make sure you are prepared with your own questions and are ready to answer their questions on a wide variety of subjects that the student government is involved in.

Mediation

You will often be required to serve as a mediator between different student groups or between students and faculty at your school. This is the most uncomfortable job that many people must deal with. Conflicts can become very stressful, so you'll need to keep a cool head and work with both sides to find a solution. Your special role as an official representative of the students can help rectify the situation.

Tips for Mediation:

1. **Get the story from both sides**: Try to understand what each side wants and why. Talk about this before a meeting between the two parties or at the very beginning of the meeting.

DON'T...

... let your ego get in the way.

... create further division.

... take sides.

2. **Gaining both sides' trust**: When a resolution needs to be established you must remain unbiased in your comments and suggestions so that each side can rely on you to properly address their concerns.

3. **Work with each side individually**: Work with the people involved to identify how much they are willing to give to make a resolution happen. When they are isolated from the opposing side they will be more forthcoming and honest about their needs.

4. **Keep your cool**: Success at helping others will depend on your ability to weigh both sides and arbitrate the disagreement in a fair and rational manner. Blowing up or getting emotional will set the discussion back or make a resolutions unreachable.

How to Work With your Team

- **Be polite**: You are in a work environment with people from many different backgrounds. Tempers can flare but it's important to stay on everyone's good side as much as possible. If you have a disagreement, resolve it immediately by talking to that person directly then move past it. You still have to work with that person in the future and ongoing conflicts will make it more stressful.

- **Don't go over someone's head**: Go through the appropriate channels of leadership whenever possible to accomplish your goal. The management structure exists for a reason, so resolve your questions or concerns with your immediate leader – that's what they are there for. Student leaders are particularly prone to being offended and having their ego bruised

- **Contribute to the discussion**: Be an active part of any discussion, especially when you have a good idea about how to proceed. Just because you're new or not as familiar with the subject matter doesn't mean your opinion doesn't matter. Everyone is in student government to make things better for the student body and frequently a fresh idea is just what the group needs.

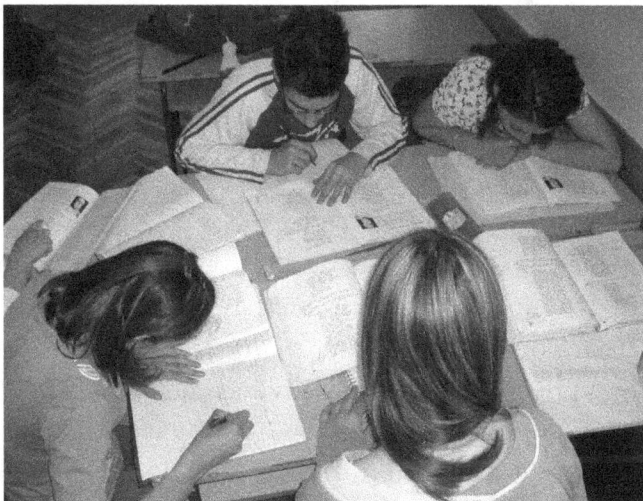

- **Volunteer often**: Getting things done is in everyone's best interest, so help as much as you can. Your goals are tied into the success of many people around you as well. You'll share in the success of other activities and you'll be able to ask for their help when you really need it in the future.

- **Deal with slackers productively**: If someone is not pulling their weight in the team, try to find out why. You can talk to them directly by approaching the situation in a positive manner: "We all want to get this project done, so what part of it are you excited about? How can you use your unique skills to contribute?" Do your best to help motivate them, and try to identify something they would get excited about so they can be part of the team.

- **Learn to disagree**: When you don't have the extra time, or something would adversely affect your project, make sure you say so in a positive way. You'll find that most things can be changed so that everyone can benefit, and it's far better than holding a grudge or sacrificing the quality of your program.

Summary

This section was focused by the typical responsibilities student government's hold with regard to governing and representing the student body. Funding for both internal program costs and managing funding for major student organization events has become a dominant function of student government activities and one of the most highly debated. Dealing with public perception of your student government is also an important aspect to deal with because it can often make or break your organization's ability to be perceived as dealing with issues competently. Also, to help understand the needs and wants of the student body it is often necessary to get information straight from the source, through issue forums, surveys and club visits. Finally, dealing with problems between groups and within your own group productively also comes to the forefront of things you'll deal with in student government.

Chapter 3: Being a Leader and Coordinating your Project

Being a leader is not just a matter of telling people what to do. You'll be required to put in work organizing the project in the background by preparing for meetings and activities. The skills in this chapter will help with the common tasks a leader will face on a regular basis.

Time Management

There are a limited number of hours in the day to juggle studies, friends and student government responsibilities. Time management skills will help you to be more effective with your time. Creating more available time for yourself is not an easy skill to develop and takes a lot of mental effort. Decide what is important to accomplish in your day and how much time you will spend on each activity. If you plan your time well you will get things done, know when you're free time is, and have more available time.

Multi-tasking is not effective: You'll feel like you're being efficient by getting a lot done at the same time, but it's not the best way to get the most effective tasks done. It may be hard but put down the text-message, close your e-mail and focus on your most important task, get it done quickly and properly then move on to the next task you need to accomplish.

Measuring Priorities

Efficient vs. Effective: Being efficient means getting a lot of work done in the quickest and most economical way, regardless of the importance of the tasks. Effectiveness on the other hand means getting the tasks done that move you closest to your goal. You could be an efficient person at putting up posters around your campus to advertise for an event. If the original project plan established that the most effective way of reaching your audience was sending out targeted e-mails to club leaders, then putting up posters may be efficient, but it is not the most effective thing to do.

Important vs. Urgent

Important tasks are similar to effective tasks in that they are critical steps that have an impact on your project or event. Your goal should be to spend your time on things that are important and not urgent. This means that you're dealing with key activities, but not at the last minute. If you don't deal with tasks when they're not urgent they can accumulate quickly and force you to deal with them right away, even if it's not convenient to do so.

Deal with items that are not urgent and not important in a disciplined way. Take care of them, but don't spend any more time on them than you have to. This includes tasks like filling out a room reservation for a meeting. Do not ignore these things completely, or they will become urgent and again force you to deal with them at an inconvenient time. You'll end up reacting to things that would have been easier to take care of earlier, like forgetting to reserve the meeting room until the day before and finding out its already booked by someone else.

The 100/80/60/40/20 Rule

When planning your week, plan 100% of your time on Monday, 80% of your time on Tuesday, and so on. Things will come up unexpectedly, so you want to leave more time open at the end of the week.

Time Tips:

- Delegate, delegate, delegate. If someone else can do a task, let them do it so you can focus on what only you can do.
- Schedule double the time you think the task will take, but try to get things done in half the time. This allows greater flexibly in your schedule.
- Focus on one of your priorities at a time and work at it until it is finished.
- Know what times of the day and week you work best to maximize your effectiveness.
- Do unpleasant tasks first thing in the morning to avoid putting them off for later in the day or forgetting them entirely.
- Put things on one list, like a to-do list or on a plan you make for your week.
- Keep copies of everything, just in case.
- File important things away immediately.
- Learn to say "no" when you just don't have time.
- Spend some time every day staying organized and at least an hour every week planning out what you need to do.
- Don't schedule every minute – plan time for the unexpected.
- Wear a watch to keep yourself on track and on schedule.

Developing Leaders
Organize Yourself out of the job

The goal is to build leaders in your team that are confident and competent. This will allow you to take on new and challenging projects yourself. This basic concept of leadership development ensures that you continue to build leaders in your group by allowing them to grow and take on parts of your job. Eventually they will replace your original position while you move into a different role.

Dividing Roles and Responsibilities

Dividing up roles allows everyone to contribute to the success of the project by being in charge of their own distinct parts. Identify the best roles for members of your team based on their unique skills. Each person responds to leadership styles and practices differently so keep that in mind when distributing tasks.

What if you like your job?

It should always be your goal to do things better and more effectively, but how can you do that when you're bogged down in the mundane parts of your job. Getting other people involved and participating will give you more time to make those improvements.

Assigning roles to your team:

- **Specialization**: Each person can become an expert in a particular element of the project. The goal is that they become the best person at doing that job by spending their time perfecting the role. For example, one member of your team could handle all media relations and begin to develop relationships with the reporters.

- **Sense of ownership**: By giving a member of your team responsibility over one aspect of the project, you allow them to become invested in its success. They'll be engaged in the project because they are making decisions and taking ownership of their responsibilities.

- **Work is Distributed**: A collaborative team will accomplish more than one person managing each person's tasks and handing out work that needs to get done. The primary leader will still have organizational work to do but the team will already know what they are responsible for.

- **Reduced Stress**: You won't have to worry as much about the small and relatively unimportant tasks getting done because they should be handled by the individuals in their respective roles. Each team member is worrying about their particular element and the team leader can focus on the overall problems.

Steps for Organizing Yourself Out of the Job:

1. Begin training new volunteers, interns, or commissioners with the basic leadership skills

2. Promote the most active team member into team leader positions and help them train the group.

3. As their skill and confidence grows, continue to train and challenge their abilities.

4. Delegate parts of your responsibilities to them until they have taken over your role.

5. Now its time to work on the next student government project: plan it out, recruit people for it, and then organize yourself out of it again.

Organizing a Training

1. **Prepare**: Creating a training program should be a task of its own. You'll want to become well versed in the topic you are teaching. Use the topics in this manual as a guideline. Bring in other sources for more in depth training on a specific topic.

2. **Bring materials**: Give your trainees something to take with them so they can reference it later. You'd be surprised at how long people hold onto good notes.

3. **Make it interactive**: When you are presenting the material ask for feedback, answers to questions, and examples from the audience. This allows the people you are training to become invested in what you are teaching. They will learn and retain more information when they are engaged in the training.

4. **Break into groups**: Have an activity as part of the training that forces individuals to use what they've just learned in a theoretical scenario. For example, if you're teaching them how to plan a project, give them a sample concert to plan in groups.

5. **Keep it short**: Trainings should be on one subject at a time, and no longer than an hour. Any longer than that and people become tired and retain less information.

Running an Effective Meeting

When you run an effective meeting it will help build a stronger team through discussion and debate, which allows for more unified agreement through building a consensus. It can also serve to share information rapidly with many people and brainstorm new ideas. You've been in meetings that are agonizingly unstructured and off track to the point where very little is accomplished. No one enjoys them and it becomes a time wasting activity.

Setting Agenda Priorities

- **Think about your goals**: What is the reason you need to have a meeting and how will this get you closer to your goals. Think ahead about how this fits into future plans. Remember: there is no point in having a meeting if it doesn't get you closer to your goal.

- **Generating Action**: For a meeting to be productive there needs to be some action generated. Plan on delegating out tasks during the meeting and setting a timeline to ensure things are completed in a timely manner.

- **Participation and Delegation**: Group participation is a must for effective meetings. Try to assign sections of the meeting to multiple people so that everyone gets a chance to speak. This helps develop new leaders by building confidence and group unity. Meeting facilitators should only talk about a quarter of the time.

- **Keeping on Time**: Put times next to each item on the agenda to make sure everyone in the meeting knows when its time to move on.

The Secret to Keeping on Track

Set times next to each agenda item with how long the group should spend on that topic. Be realistic because you're going to need to stick to the schedule for the most part. This lets you know when its time to move on and focuses the conversation on only the most important topics, rather than getting sidetracked on unimportant matters.

Guidelines for the meeting

- **Preparation for the meeting**: Spend as much time preparing for the meeting as the meeting is set to last. Ask yourself questions like: Is the location of the room convenient? Is the room big enough? Is it set up for discussion? Do you have a whiteboard for brainstorming? Sign-in contact sheet? All the necessary materials? Refreshments or socializing? Set and generally agreed upon agenda?

- **Know your goals**: The agenda should clearly lay out the goals for the meeting and establish an atmosphere that makes everyone comfortable. Figure out what discussions need to happen and what decisions need to be made.

- **Prepare all participants**: Everyone coming to the meeting should have a basic sense of the goals, how they will participate and who else will be in attendance. Meeting facilitators should have a sense of what needs to come out of the meeting and who is best suited to do each task so that they can guide the conversation.

- **Anticipate the problems**: The most difficult part of running a successful meeting is dealing with the dynamics of the attendees. The meeting facilitator needs to be encouraging discussion, laying out summarized opinions clearly, as well as making people feel comfortable enough to talk.

- **Put goals in context**: While most people in the meeting will have some grasp of the purpose of the meeting, it's always good to reiterate why everyone is there. Put the goal of the meeting and any major problems into context of the larger picture so the newer people know what's going on. This is a great way to reenergize everyone.

- **Recap after the meeting**: Take a few minutes after the agenda wraps up to talk casually with the people who were in the meeting and ask what worked and didn't work well. Use these pros and cons to decide what to change for the next meeting.

- **Follow up after the meeting**: Some time after the meeting is over check in with the attendees: thank everyone for coming and make sure delegated tasks are happening. This is essential to keep things moving outside the meeting.

Simple Legislative & Parliamentary Procedures

Your school probably has some type of legislative body as part of the student government, whether it's a student senate or a council of the elected executives. These elected bodies, for the most part, operate using a form of parliamentary procedures which ensures that the meeting can be run effectively. Having a specific set of rules to govern who can speak and when motions can be brought up for debate helps to guarantee that everyone gets a chance to speak and that the meeting proceeds in an orderly fashion. Parliamentary procedure can become quite complex and only a brief explanation based on Roberts Rules of Order Newly Revised will be included here.

Terms

- **Bylaws**: These are the rules that govern the legislative body to ensure that all procedures are set before an important decision is made and that everyone knows the same rules.

- **Minutes**: This is a written record of the meeting and includes motions, vote totals and the major arguments made during the meeting.

- **Quorum**: Is the number of members that must be present at the meeting for any substantial decisions to be made. This ensures that business may proceed despite a certain number of absentees, as long as the minimum number is reached. This number can typically be found in the bylaws for the organization.

- **Chair**: This is the presiding officer of the meeting. He or she is chosen to keep the meeting in order, take motions and determine the order of the debate. This person is typically a facilitator of the meeting, but may vote in accordance with the bylaws.

- **Motion**: A motion is a suggested action or request made by a member of the board after obtaining the recognition of the chair. These are agreed as statements with a common meaning that every member of the board knows and understands. Motions typically proceed as requested unless there is an objection, where a vote will be required for the motion to proceed.

Typical Order of the Meeting:

1. Call the meeting to order

2. Review and approval of the past meeting minutes

3. Approval of the meeting agenda

4. Unfinished business from the previous meeting

5. New business to be discussed at the current meeting

6. Committee reports

7. Officer reports

8. Announcements and Adjournment

Types of Voting

Unanimous Consent: This method passes a motion with unanimous approval without a vote count unless there is an objection. In the case of an objection a different type of vote will be required. Acclamation is typically used for simple votes on non-confrontational topics.

Roll Call: All members will be required to vote yes or no without abstentions and their specific choice will be recorded with their name. Typically voting will go around the room and each member may pass either once or twice before they are required to submit their final vote.

Majority: This is a set amount of the members currently in attendance that are required to vote in favor of the motion either by standing up, raising their hands, submitting a ballot or some other way of indicating their vote choice. The most common is a simple majority, where the required vote is just over 50% of attendance. Another type is a 2/3rds vote for more important votes like changing the constitution or bylaws.

Standard Motions and Order of Debate:

Person A: "I move that ___" and clearly phrase your recommended course of action, proposed legislation, or request.

Person B: "Second" to agree with the motion put forth.

Chair: "The proposal on the floor is to ___." The chair restates the proposal so that everyone can clearly hear and understand.

Person A: "I move to debate current proposal for ___ minutes." This moves the proposal into the debating stage and puts a cap on extraneous and unimportant discussions. Each persons speaking time can also be set at this time.

Person B: "Second"

Chair: "Debate is open on the current proposal for ___ minutes." Without objections the debate is open. The chair may create a list of members who wish to speak on the issue.

- Debate proceeds until time has been reached. During this time members can speak, amendments can be proposed and voted on, and additional motions can be made such as extending or ending debate time. -

Chair: "Time is up. Are there any motions on the floor?" This lets people know that another motion is needed to move the meeting along.

Person A: "I move to call this proposal to question." This proposes a vote on the current proposal. If you have a special request for a type of voting you should also specify that in the motion.

Person B: "Second."

Chair: "The proposal to ___ has been called to a vote. All those in favor ___?" The chair instructs the group how to indicate their choice (hand raise, ballot, etc).

Chair "All those opposed? Abstaining?"

Chair: "The proposal passes (or fails). The results are __ for, __ against, and __ abstaining." State the results so all members know and so that it can be recorded in the minutes.

Chair: "Are there any other motions on the floor? The next order of business is ___ " The chair opens the floor to any other requests before proceeding to the next point on the agenda.

Making Amendments

Person A: "I move to amend the current proposal so that the section that currently reads ___ will be changed to read ___." Stating the section to be changed and how it will be changed allows all members to follow along and be clear about the change.

Chair: "All those in favor of amending the section that reads ___ to ___? All those opposed? Abstaining?" The chair restates the amendment and calls for a vote.

Basic Motions and Uses

	Requires Recognition	Requires a Second	Debatable	Amendable	Vote Required	May be Reconsidered
Adjourn	Y	Y	N	N	Majority	N
Recess	Y	Y	N	Y	Majority	N
Limit or Extend Debate	Y	Y	N	Y	2/3rds	Y
Postpone	Y	Y	Y	Y	Majority	Y
Refer to a committee	Y	Y	Y	Y	Majority	Y
Amend	Y	Y	Y	Y	Majority	Y
General Motions	Y	Y	Y	Y	Majority	Y
Reconsider Previous Motion	N	Y	Y	N	Majority	N
Override Committee Decision	Y	Y	Y	Y	2/3rds or Majority	Only negative votes
Requests (Inquires, Procedure, Urgent non business problems)	N	N	N	N	---	N
Suspend the Normal Rules	N	N	N	N	2/3rds	N
Withdraw a Motion	Y	Y	N	N	Majority	Only negative votes
Objection to Consideration	N	N	N	N	2/3rds	Only negative votes

Summary

Developing the skills you need to be a leader in your area of responsibility is at the core of this chapter. Managing your time effectively can mean the difference between accomplishing your goals or getting bogged down in irrelevant, time consuming activities. You can also boost the effectiveness of your project by identifying and completing the most important tasks first as well as delegating tasks to other members of your team. These tactics require more effort on your part but help generate more of an effect in the end by freeing up your time and getting the important things done quickly. Additionally, the ability to run meetings in an effective manner is an important skill to develop because most of the action for your group will be generated out of meetings.

Chapter 4: Get the Word Out with Messaging, Advertising, and News Media

At some point in time you'll need to tell the student body about the project you're working on. A great idea without the support of great communication skills will not get very far. By using these techniques to get the word out you'll be able to create a winning message to grab people's attention with a variety of advertising methods and media attention.

Creating an Engaging Message

Whether it is a concert or getting students registered to vote, you need to reach people who are not paying attention. Creating a good message will help you custom tailor ideas of your project be the most effective in reaching your target groups. The ideal message will address your target's needs by articulating the points of difference and the unique benefits. Avoid traits that are similar because you don't need to reiterate what someone will already assume about your activity. You can also use your knowledge about the competing activities to think of creative methods to present your message.

> **Structuring a quick action statement**
>
> 1. Present the Problem
>
> 2. Propose the Solution
>
> 3. Explain how your target group can help

Steps to Message Crafting:

1. **Defining your issue or event**: What is your vision for your project? What is the objective? Why does it matter?

2. **Defining the target**: Who are you targeting with your message and why? Who will benefit from your actions? Who this message will be directed at: Students, the news media, a federal legislator?

3. **Connect with your target's needs**: What does your target group need? Focus on specific qualities of your issue but also include general needs that require their attention like school work or paying rent.

4. **Identify elements competing for the target's attention**: Who and what are the competitors for their attention and time? Include all that come to mind.

5. **Set Points of Similarity**: What qualities make your issue or event similar to others. These are things that people will expect from the category of events or issues you're working on.

6. **Recognize the Points of Difference**: What aspect makes it different than the nearest competing activity or from the base assumption about your campaign?

7. **Identify Unique Benefits**: What are the best benefits of your project, issue or event. This includes the strongest points from the previous steps. Present a solution to the needs of the target while articulating the points that make the solution special. Identify the unique benefits that give you a basic and strong statement you can use as a template for your messaging. Alter the message to suit your needs as different situations arise.

Double Check for Jargon: Always have someone outside of the team check your message. Advertising campaigns have fallen drastically short of expectations because the message didn't work for the target group.

Sample Message Craft

Example: Student Academic Input Campaign

1. **Defining the issue**: Students should have a **say in decisions made about the academic content** of their classes and the requirements of their major. The goal is to have at least one student seat on every academic decision making board on this campus.

2. **Defining the target**: The targets will be the **deans of each college** and **board chairs** of each committee. Both the **academic leaders and the students will benefit** from the outcome of this campaign.

3. **Connect with your target's needs**: Specifically to this campaign, the professors are seeking a **diversity of views and ideas** that allow them to make the **best decision about the quality** of the academic content of their classes. Other needs include satisfying their **academic curiosity** in their area of study, **satisfying their job and teaching** responsibilities as well as their **families**.

4. **Identify competing elements**: College professors are being pulled by the requirements of their **classes**, the **teaching assistants**, and especially **research** for their area of study. Other **personal commitments** inside and outside the university are also vying for their attention.

5. **Set points of similarity**: This is a student campaign trying to achieve **greater rights** for their follow students. Students want **freedom and control** over their academic future.

6. **Recognize the points of difference**: This campaign is different because it focuses on addressing the problem that students don't get an education they **need for their future pursuits**.

7. **Identify unique benefits**: This course of action **benefits the professors** by giving them **important feedback** and **original suggestions**, allowing them to be **more effective teachers** and for the students to get an education **focused on their needs**.

Messaging Missteps:

You may have the best of intentions when trying to use powerful elements to define your message, but the following are examples of errors that can occur.

- **Student Government Lingo** — Ex: Mentioning SAIC, an acronym for the campaign that people are unfamiliar with.

- **Unrelated Statements** — Ex: Making an analogy to the civil rights movement during a campaign for a new events center

- **Words & Phrases Associated with other things** — Claiming that the administration is waterboarding the students by excluding them from participating in the academic board meetings.

- **Boring or Passive Words** — Ex: This idea is good because professors can hear what students have to say, which makes them better teachers and so students can get a good education. (See the improved version in #7 in the example)

Getting Your Project Noticed: Visibility
Advertising Campaigns

Ad campaigns let people know about what is going on around campus. Advertising is used to tell people about events going on and ways they can get more information. It is nearly impossible to generate any action with passive visibility, such as telling people to call into a local politician to influence his or her vote on an education issue.

Putting up posters is the most traditional method for advertising on college campuses. Most school have designated areas full of posters about all the events going on. This makes it important that you come up with creative ways to get your message out to your target groups. Consider whether the specific method you choose is cost effective. How many people are going to get the message for every dollar you spend on the advertising method?

The trade-off between the time investment in creating the type of advertising, the monetary cost, and the audience it will be seen by. This is the difference between coming up with a creative idea that takes a lot of labor and time investment but doesn't cost a lot of money versus spending a large amount of money to have someone design and print a flier or poster that gets done quickly and easily. An example would be hand drawing murals on posters – each poster takes an extremely long time to create, which limits the number of people who will see it, although it does draw more attention than the average poster. Student governments tend to err on the side of spending more money rather than spending more time to create advertising, primarily due to tight deadlines and frequent events.

Making Use of Color Schemes and Thematic Elements

Creating a unified color scheme gets your advertising recognized more often than others. If people begin to see a set of similar red posters in a sea of grey or white posters they will begin to notice that your ads stand out. The goal of having a unified theme is that student will associate the repeated visuals with your message.

It helps if you can create a theme that flows through your advertising campaign that people will identify with your issue or event. This could be an iconic figure, a Viking for example, or some specific and unique image you want to associate with your initiative. The best theme will be easily recognizable and be able to communicate your message in visual form. Keep it simple. You want people to make quick links between your message and your theme.

Another method uses references or associations with popular brands, like car companies or corporations, and pop culture, like popular movies or public figures. This is less recommended, as your ad campaign then becomes dependent on the success or failure of the brand you choose. However, you may not be able to use it because of copyright laws. It's best to check before using an existing brand as inspiration.

Design Tips

When you are designing any kind of visual advertisement, from posters to fliers to e-mails, keep in mind these basic principles.

- **The Visual Grab**: The grab gives the viewer a reason to keep looking and learning more. This could be your eye catching image, a captivating slogan, or unique color that draws people's attention to the advertisement.

- **Visual Order Matters**: What do you want to be noticed first? This could be something that your target group will pay attention to and keep reading where others won't. It's typically the slogan and visual. Once you've got someone reading make sure they see things in the proper order. Place elements from top to bottom or left to right, but also arrange the design by font size and visuals.

- **Don't Jump Around**: Make it as easy as possible for the viewer to read what you want to communicate. Keep it simple and ordered. Don't put the time and date of an event in visual order before the statement saying what the event is, because people will lose track in the split second they glance at the poster.

- **Be Unique**: Nothing hurts your advertising campaign like being completely average and thus, unnoticeable. Strive to make your campaign stand out. Go through the message crafting again to come up with ideas.

Estimated Cost Per View:

Online: <$0.01

Posters: $0.04

Fliers: $0.10

Newspaper: $0.18

T-Shirts: $0.30

Active Visibility Events

Events with the sole purpose of making someone aware of an issue or event have a specific set of rules to follow. (See Tabling for more info on logistics of visibility events)

- **Make Yourself Stand Out**: Nothing generates attention like screaming for it. You want to be noticeable, so use bright colors, striking images, or something out of the ordinary like having someone playing an acoustic guitar in front of your table. Make sure to reinforce a positive impression of your event or campaign.

- **Visibility Events Need Visuals**: Draw the attention of both students and media to your cause through striking visuals. This could be a prop that has a unique connection with the issue or event, like a giant walking textbook for a textbooks affordability issue or everyone dressed in Halloween costumes while advertising for the annual campus Halloween festival.

- **Be Active**: Drawing attention is difficult, so the more excited and energized you and your volunteers are the better everything will look. Talk to people face to face rather than sitting behind a table, have people move around to make the event more exciting.

Types of Advertising Methods

Ways to Boost Visibility		
Try a different shape: Make posters round, or triangular, or even blob-like. It doesn't matter what shape it is as long as it stands out	Use a unique color: Nobody else is using fuchsia posters? If your event or issue won't suffer from being associated with bright pink then go for it.	Print glossy posters: If you get your posters professionally printed they'll stand out against hand-made club posters and they'll convey the image of legitimacy and authority.
Professionalism helps: The more legitimate the flier looks, the more someone is going to take the time to look at it. This includes using card stock, glossy printing, well designed messages and visuals.	Keep it simple: Only include relevant information and stick to your message. The longer it is the less it will be read it.	Hand it out at relevant functions: Get to your core audience quickly by selecting appropriate locations like club meetings or relevant events.
Catchy without color: Most ads appear in black and white, so think of an interesting grab that will work without color. You need your ad to stand out against other ads and the standard newspaper content.	Make a deal: Work out a deal with your campus newspaper for ideal ad placement and a potential discount.	Take out a whole page: A whole page makes your ad unavoidable. It is usually so expensive that it is only reserved for once or twice a year.
Designate event or project staff: T-shirts can be useful to identify the students in charge so people can ask them questions.	Double your views: Remember that T-shirts are two sided, so take advantage of getting views from both directions.	Unified color scheme: Make the t-shirts the same unique color to make them catchy. Students will associate the different parts of the campaign together.
Be straight and to the point: Keep your message concise despite having more space for your message. Don't beat around the bush. People will just ignore the message.	Use relevant mailing lists or groups: Sending an e-mail to an appropriate mailing list or group will boost the number of people who read the message.	Start an interest group: Create a group specifically for your event or issue so you know everyone in it is interested.

Type	Description	Pros	Cons
Posters	~It's the tried and true form of advertising on campus. ~Includes: butcher paper posters colored with markers, photocopied ads, or glossy professionally printed posters.	~It's simple, easy to produce and relatively cheep. ~You tend to get a large amount of views per dollar because of the volume of students walking by.	~Students see them but don't pay attention because there are so many. ~It's hard to reach your specific target because everyone is exposed to the poster.
Fliers	~Small informational papers passed out individually. ~Anything from informational pamphlets to basic info about an event	~Cheep and easy to mass produce. ~It gets into student's hands	~Student will throw it away without looking at it especially when other groups are handing out fliers too. ~Causes litter that is difficult to pick up.
News Ads	~Advertising space in your campus newspaper.	~You can reach a large number of students at one time.	~A small ad costs up to a couple hundred dollars. ~You can't control placement. ~People will not necessarily see it.
T-Shirts	~Inform people by letting them read the shirt as they are walking around or sitting in class	~Students see it in addition to/instead of posters. ~You can bring into class. ~If someone is interested they can ask for more info.	~They are almost prohibitively expensive for mass advertising: 20-30 shirts can cost hundreds of dollars.
Online	~Using methods like e-mail, websites, and instant messenger to communicate with other students (See Online Mobilization)	~Free advertising through mailing lists, target website ads and networking websites. ~Groups on networking sites get you to your targets	~Any form of online communication can be dismissed easily. It's difficult to ensure that people will see it.

Generating Media Attention

The media is an incredibly powerful tool. If you can master media relations it will help achieve your goals, reach out to allies, recruit supporters, let the student body know what is going on, and get a movement going. The news media is the main conduit through which local, state and national government officials communicate with their constituents. With that in mind, being able to work effectively with the media as a representative of the student body will help push your causes forward.

Elements of a good media plan: (See Message Crafting)

1. **Keep it simple**: Short and direct is the key when creating a media message. Print and TV news reporters are always short on time so communicate your event and message in as few sentences as possible. They are far more likely to listen that way.

2. **Grab their attention**: Differentiate your story from all the other stories that news reporters are hearing about. Give them a reason to pursue what you have to say. Figure out what makes your event or campaign unique and communicate it.

3. **Timeliness:** Your story needs to be presented as an urgent problem in order to get their attention. Communicate that sense of urgency in order to generate the story when you need it. This is the reason they'll pursue your story now rather than forgetting about it because it happens months from now.

4. **Photo Op**: A picture is worth a thousand words and media professionals love good visuals to connect with their stories, especially involving TV or print stories.

The Myth about the Media

The news media is a great ally to have on your side no matter what you're working on. They can pave the way to your success or leave your issues stuck. Even if you don't think you need media coverage to push your campaign forward, it never hurts to submit a celebratory piece to the paper so that students at your school can simply know what is going on and that you're working hard for them.

Steps to Getting Media Attention

1. **Create or find a major action event to generate a story**: Reporters like action. Use your event or a related event to spring board your issue or event into the press' attention. Ex: "In conjunction with the major congressional committee vote on student grants, we're launching our own campaign to promote student financial aid with…"

2. **Creating your materials**

   a. **Create a media list (newspapers, TV news, radio, magazines, blogs):** Include the station, type of media, contact reporter if possible, phone, fax, and e-mail.

   b. **Write a Press Advisory**: This is the press' invitation to your event so make it catchy and engaging.

   c. **Write a Press Release**: This is the ideal story you'd like them to publish. They'll use a lot of the material you provide in the press release in their article.

   d. **Questions and Answers**: Write out any and all questions you think reporters will ask. Attach answers to each one based off your message, press advisory and release. This keeps everything consistent.

   Timeline for Media:

   One Week before, 8am-9am:
   > Submit Press Advisory
   > First round media calls

   Two days before, 8am-9am:
   > Second round press advisory
   > Second round media calls

   Day of, before the event:
   > Third round press advisory

   Day of, after the event:
   > Submit Press Release
   > Follow-up media calls

   Day after, 8am-9am
   > Contact unreached media outlets

3. **Submitting a Press Advisory**: Submit the press advisory by fax and e-mail one week before the action event is to take place to give the reporters plenty of time to put it in their schedules. Send it again two days before the event and again the morning of. Send it early in the morning, between 8am and 9am. They'll see it before they get distracted with other deadlines later in the day.

4. **Contacting the Media**: Call immediately following your submission of the press advisory. Give them a brief overview of the event and ask if they received the advisory. It puts it on their radar and differentiates your fax from all the other ones coming in. Also do a follow up call two days before the event and the morning of. Again, contact members of the press between 8 and 9 am.

5. **Follow-up Communication and Press Release**: Follow up with both the reporters that attended the event and especially the ones who didn't. Just because they didn't come doesn't mean they aren't interested, they may just have been busy. This follow-up should include answering any additional questions they may have and asking about their desire to publish the story. Be insistent!

6. **Build a relationship with the press**: Establishing a relationship with members of the press can be a great benefit and will help get positive coverage in the future. If you keep providing them with interesting stories to cover they'll be grateful.

Avoid the Worst Press

Be Careful: Sometimes reporters will try to bait you into say something you shouldn't so they can write their own version of the story. Pay attention to why they are asking certain questions.

Stay on Message: Keep to your message no matter what. If a reporter asks an odd question, answer it in a way that draws the answer back into the topic of the event without giving away any compromising quotes.

Mind your Surroundings: If reporters are around don't talk about anything other than the event or the subject of the event. Don't let them quote you saying something potentially inappropriate.

What Happens when there is a Car Chase at the same time as your event?

Despite your best efforts, sometimes no one will come to a press event and sometimes your stories just won't get covered. There are a lot of other events are going on at the time. Just try again next time.

Press Advisory

University of Colorado, Colorado Springs

Student Government Association

NEWS ADVISORY

FOR IMMEDIATE RELEASE: CONTACT:

Monday, May 5, 2008, 10 AM MT   Jim Jackson, 468-648-9658, jjackson@uccs.edu

Michelle Nguyen, 468-863-9782, mnyuyen@uccs.edu

CONSERVATION CONCERT SEEKS TO URGE UCCS CAMPUS TO GO GREEN

UCCS Student Government puts on a concert with local bands and campus speakers to lobby school administrators to use solar energy to help power the campus

WHO: Jameson Dow, Professor, Head of the Environmental Analysis Department, UCCS

Paula Sheen, Executive Vice President, UCCS Student Government Association

Emilio Martinez, Conservation Students of Colorado, UCCS Chapter

Student Bands - Sewer Monkeys, The Scribes, Advocates of Indecision

WHAT: The University of Colorado, Colorado Springs Student Government Association is partnering with Conservation Students of Colorado to put on a concert to rally support for solar energy on campus. Thousands of UCCS students are expected to attend to hear the music, visit the booths advocating for various environmental issues, and eat food being sold by campus organizations. The Conservation Concert seeks to put pressure on Chancellor Miller to take action on making the campus more environmentally sustainable by implementing a policy to put solar panels on roofs of new and existing buildings on campus.

WHEN: 12:00pm – 3:30pm, Thursday, May 15th

WHERE: On the steps of the University Center, University of Colorado, Colorado Springs {Directions: Take Austin Bluffs Parkway towards the UCCS campus and turn into Parking Lot 3. Use the visitor parking spaces. Signs will guide you to the University Center}

VISUALS: Thousands of students will be gathered at the steps the University Center to hear the concert and speakers. 15 booths will also fill the area selling food and providing informational materials.

More information can be found at www.uccs.edu/SGA/ConservationConcert

###

{Put your logo or letterhead here}

NEWS ADVISORY

FOR IMMEDIATE RELEASE:

[Date advisory sent to press]

CONTACT: [Full Name, Phone #, E-mail]

[Catchy headline]

[Subtitle explaining the headline]

WHO: [List prominent speakers, participants and organizations taking part]

WHAT: [2-3 descriptive sentences about the event]

WHEN: [Date and time of event]

WHERE: [Where the event will take place. Include brief but descriptive directions for anyone to get there and where to park]

VISUALS: [Describe exciting photo ops for the press, anything relevant they can take a picture of or shoot video footage of]

More information can be found at [website address].

[Indicates end of message]

Press Release

Ohio State University

Undergraduate Student Government

NEWS RELEASE

FOR IMMEDIATE RELEASE: CONTACT:

Monday October 20th, 9 AM CT   Laura Merino, 614-283-5512, president@usg.osu.edu

Sean Williams, 614-661-8462, swilliams@osu.edu

STUDENTS, ADMINISTRATION CLASH OVER USE OF EVENTS CENTER

OSU Undergraduate Student Government says student organizations sidelined in getting time, space in events center over the last two years since the center opened.

The Ohio State University Undergraduate Student Government announced it is beginning an official investigation into the usage policies of the student fee funded Student Events Complex following a series of complaints by student organizations not being able to get time or space to put on their own events for the campus. Student government representatives will be seeking documents and records from the center to corroborate these complaints as well as meeting with campus administrators to discuss the problem.

"These are facilities and programs that students have voted to fund and we have every right to demand they be run effectively," said Jefferson Vu, a concerned student.

The Latino Student Union at Ohio State University for example regularly puts on a culture festival every year in the fall with almost one thousand students in attendance. They have sought to hold the event in the larger facilities of the Student Event Complex but have been repeatedly denied.

"It is unfortunate that many of the clubs on campus have not been allowed to put on events in the center even though that was the original intention. They could be so much bigger, attract more students and provide more diversity to campus activities," Student President of the Campus Culture Coalition, Sean Williams said.

The Director of the Student Events Complex Jacqueline Martin cites conflicts over athletic events and outside events as well as the need to generate revenue for the facility, "We're trying our best to accommodate everyone involved, and there are so many groups to consider."

[Your logo or letterhead]

NEWS RELEASE

FOR IMMEDIATE RELEASE:

[Date release sent to press]

CONTACT:

[Full Name, Phone #, E-mail]

[Full Name, Phone #, E-mail]

[Headline, short and descriptive]

[Subtitle explaining the headline]

[Describe the event that just happened with a brief explanation of why its significant]

[Include a quote from a supportive student or community member explaining the situation]

[Personal story about the event including a short quote]

[Quote and explanation about the event from your organization. Describe what action needs to be taken or why the action is justified]

[Include an additional explanation or outline information as needed]

From the information already compiled by the Undergraduate Student Government, the Athletics department uses the space nearly 70% of the time, where as student clubs and organizations are only able to use it 17% of the time, with the remainder going to concerts and events from off campus.

[Explain telling statistics to back up the story]

"We're conducting this investigation to get to the bottom of the student's concern. This facility is student funded and as such should be used in a manner that is appropriate for student needs," Student Government President Laura Merino said. "The athletic events are important for our campus, but the administration shouldn't loose sight of student organizations needs either. We're doing our best to work with Jacqueline Martin to come to the best outcome that will be acceptable to both campus administrators and the student organizations we represent."

[Additional straight and to the point quote to summarize the initiative/action]

The Undergraduate Student Government will be pursuing this investigation over the coming months in order to have the data needed to find a solution. They will also be working with a number of student organizations to help them get their events into the facility. Meetings are being held over the coming weeks to address student concerns.

[What your organization is doing to continue the initiative/action]

The final report from the Undergraduate Student Government is expected to be release by the end of November.

More information can be found at [website address for organization or campaign].

More information can be found at http://usg.osu.edu

The Undergraduate Student Government is the elected governing body of the students at Ohio State University, and is charged with representing student interests, working with campus administrators and communicating with the community around campus in Columbus.

[Describe your organization in one sentence]

###

###[Indicates end of message]

Summary

Effectively communicating your ideas and issues will go great lengths towards reaching your goals. The first step is creating a message that will communicate the core ideas of your program in a concise manner and allow you to make use of thematic elements to help boost visibility. Once you've identified your message you can begin to strategize about how best to communicate that message, through using different types of advertising campaigns like posters, fliers, newspaper ads, t-shirts and on-line mechanisms, or using the news media to get the word out. Your campus newspapers can be a great way to communicate with the student body. Cultivate your relationship with members of the press and provide them with easy opportunities to generate stories that you need to create a successful program.

Chapter 5: Getting Connected and Building a Coalition

Frequently, your own team in student government will not have access to all the volunteers, skills or people you need to achieve you goals. It helps to bring in other people and groups to help facilitate your goals and to help them achieve theirs.

Coalition Building

Getting students involved from different facets of the campus is a way to get the depth and breadth of experience you need when organizing an issue campaign or a major event. This adds to your ability to mobilize volunteers, get the word out to interested parties and boost the image of the event. For example, if you want to put on a festival for Cinco de Mayo you should consider partnering with your campus' Latino student organizations with the knowledge and connections to get it done.

Steps for Building a Coalition

1. **Identify your allies**: Figure out which organizations or departments would benefit from participating and which ones you feel would contribute the most to your success.

2. **Figure out roles**: Similar to the way you identify who on your team would best be able to handle certain projects, figure out which of your allies you'd ideally like to have take on parts of the project.

3. **Meet to brainstorm**: Brainstorming is a great way to get people invested in an event or campaign because each person and organization is coming up with ideas and contributing to the overall image of the project.

4. **Make the coalition collaborative**: Once you've met with the groups once or twice you can begin to build an organizational structure to identify each of the group's roles and determine how decisions are made for the coalition.

Getting the rest of student government on board

In most student governments there is a difference of opinions. Dealing with many teams, departments, and offices makes bringing the entire organization together around one issue difficult. When you're working on a difficult issue or campaign that has student government divided you'll have a lot more work to do trying to get everyone on board. You'll need to turn to your lobbying skills to convince people of the merit of your side.

Lobbying

No matter where you are in student government: volunteer, commissioner, elected legislator or executive, at some point you'll have to convince the elected members of your student government to take action. This could be in the form of passing a piece of legislation through the legislative branch or convincing the student government president to take action on an issue. While you'll have to lobby your own student government most of the time, you can also use many of these tips to lobby your local elected representatives.

Tips for lobbying success

1. **Build a personal connection**: Make an effort to introduce yourself to legislative decision makers. A personal connection goes a long way towards getting someone to listen to the benefits of your proposal. Take the time to ask them about other issues you are working on to get a feel for their response.

2. **Do you research**: Everyone in student government has some connection to everyone else, so ask the students you know about the individuals you want to convince. Use your contacts to do research on where people stand on an issue or where your initiative might get hung up. Know which pros and cons of your issue they will bring up. Going in with the facts is indispensable.

3. **Talk to decision makers in person**: Discuss you issue with them and see what concerns they have. Take those opinions into account when you want to pass a bill. You may not decide to address their concerns, but at least you'll be prepared for their arguments.

4. **Identify elite decision makers**: Many elected officials listen to an influential member of the legislative council or student government. Get these people on your side, they tend to carry more votes than just their individual contribution. Don't get on the bad side of the elite decision makers because their influence may be enough to kill your initiative in its tracks.

5. **Be prepared**: Once you've gotten a feel for the political climate around a certain issue, ensure you have enough confirmed votes to pass your initiative before it is brought up for a vote. This way you'll limit the degree to which the vote could turn unexpectedly against you.

6. **Have an ally introduce the legislation**: If you are not a member of the decision making board find one strong ally to champion your cause. This person must be able to clearly articulate the nuances of your initiative and know where it can and cannot be compromised.

Networking

Networking is about building mutually beneficial relationships with people who you can help and who can in turn help you. Most of the information you'll get is not from reading the newspaper or keeping up with the official releases from the campus administration. You'll get it from your peers. That's where the most current and relevant information is.

Suggested Networking Strategies

- **Get out and walk around**: Walking around the campus has many benefits aside from feeling refreshed. You'll run into an old acquaintance you wouldn't have taken the time to talk to otherwise or happen upon an administrator you've been dying to set up a meeting with.

- **Be a socialite**: Go to different types of events that will expose you to students on campus who care about very different activities than you do. It's important to know what all students are feeling and what they care about, not just the ones you hang out with or who share your values.

- **Go to meetings of clubs**: Most clubs never shy away from new people at their meetings. Interact with these students,. They are heavily involved in the campus and may have an interesting insight or two.

- **Share what interests you**: One thing that connects people the best is talking about their mutual passions. Share yours and find out what drives other students. You'll be well on your way to building your network and staying connected to the pulse of the campus.

- **Listen to everyone**: Each person comes from a different background which gives them a unique perspective on a current issue. Be careful not to exclusively listen to your friends or your work group because it may give you a narrow vision of the world.

Power Mapping and Elite Allies

Elite Allies are important to secure because they can bring many people to the table that would not otherwise come or be able to make high level decisions themselves. These are people who have influence, and you want to partner with them. Help them participate in an important action and have that action succeed through their participation.

Power Mapping

1. Identify the important people you need to influence based on your plan.

2. Create a chart showing their relationships with each other. Include any friends or associates of these people that you know about.

3. Figure out who the lowest level person on the chart is that could get you what you want.

4. Work with this person to rectify your issue, and allow sufficient time for them to bring the problem to their superiors as needed.

5. Work with whatever person is handling the issue as it moves around within a particular department or as the issue rises through the ranks. Follow the lead of the people you're working with.

6. When you run into a problem, use your chart again to identify people who may be able to favorably influence the person who needs to make a decision.

7. Use your chart to keep track of who you've spoken what about which topics so you don't get confused.

Respecting Ranks

Always start with the lowest person who can help you and work your way up from there. Frequently a decision lies much lower down the totem pole than you think, and that person often has more time to help you.

Don't idly jump levels or go straight to the top: You can burn a lot of bridges by going over people's heads unnecessarily. Put in your due diligence working on the appropriate level and if you have evidence of them disregarding your concerns then go to their boss.

Finding and Being a Mentor

Mentors are very knowledgeable individuals that will help teach you what they know from years of personal experience. A mentor can be anyone from an older and more experienced student to an adult with years of experience in your field on interest. This is a person you identify with and have a special connection with. Mentors have a lot of impact on helping you understand you own priorities and getting you connected into the right places.

Why Mentors are Important

- **Knowledge**: Mentors have been through many problems that you are just beginning to encounter. If you are able to ask the right questions you'll learn how to master skills more quickly than most people. Mentors can help by going over problems you are having or issues you are facing and give you suggestions of actions to pursue.

- **Connections**: Mentors are connected in a wide network of people they've met and worked with over the years. Be specific about what you are interested in or want to pursue and they will have suggestion of people to talk to.

- **Support**: When you don't need anything except some motivation, a mentor can be invaluable in offering comments to get you back on track. Because they have been through a wide range of problems before, they are well equipped to give you positive feedback for your situation.

Become a Mentor

Just as important as finding a mentor to help you through your most difficult problems and motivational challenges, you can provide the same service to other students in student government. Its important to share your unique knowledge with other students as well as foster leadership within your organization. By passing along your experience you help build a stronger student government, equipped to deal with more complex problems in the future.

Summary

This chapter focuses on building a network of administrators, student leaders and student government members with the purpose of benefiting each other and the common goals. Coalition building brings groups of like-minded organizations with a variety of skills and focuses together in order to accomplish a goal. Despite student government being one organization it typically has a great diversity of opinions about how things should be done, so it's important to be able to connect with people from your own student government to ensure the group participation you need to accomplish your objectives. Keeping connected to other students and faculty at your school will also add to your project by giving you an insight into different aspects of the campus and conduits to people you need on your side. Helping others is just as important to creating a balanced relationship as receiving help yourself.

Chapter 6: Time to Mobilize the Student Body

Some projects will require you to run a person to person, or grassroots, campaign to influence students and mobilize them to take action. You can use a combination of methods to accomplish your goals. Speak to students in person on the main stretch of campus at a table, go to their classroom to make a short announcement, and follow up with them through calls and online methods.

The Discounting Rule

You need to know how to estimate how many people you will need to reach to successfully reach your goals. This is a core component of planning for the success of your project. Below is a set of formulas you can use to help you estimate what you'll need to do to accomplish your goals for both mobilization and recruitment. Work backwards from your eventual objective to identify the intermediate targets you need to get there. For example, if you want to recruit 20 new volunteers for a voter registration drive, you need 40 students to say yes to do it. To get those 40 people you'll need to at least talk to 80 people. This means you'll need to get 160 people's contact information through one of the following methods.

Tabling for Petitions or Pledges

$$\frac{[\text{Confirmed Signatures}]}{15 \text{ per hour}} = [\text{Person-hours}]$$

$$\frac{[\text{Person-hours}]}{[\text{Total Available Hours}]} = [\text{People per hour}]$$

Class Presentations

$$\frac{[\text{Contact Goal}]}{.15 \text{ (percent of the class)}} = [\text{Students to speak to}]$$

$$\frac{[\text{Students to speak to}]}{[\text{Average class size}]} = [\text{Number of Classes}]$$

E-mail Lists

$[\text{Contact Goal}] \times 400 \text{ E-mails per view} = [\text{People to E-mail}]$

On-line Common Interest Groups

$[\text{Contact Goal}] \times 40 \text{ Members per response} = [\text{People needed in the group}]$

[ ] Denotes a number you put in or get out of the equation

Recruitment

Whether you need to get volunteers, interns or commissioners involved in student government at the beginning of the year or you need a bunch of new people to help with an amazing event you are putting on later in the academic year, these tried and true recruitment strategies will benefit you every time.

Contact Calling

[Recruitment Goal] $\times$ 2 $=$ [Confirmed Yeses]

[Confirmed Yeses] $\times$ 2 $=$ [Spoken with]

[Spoken with] $\times$ 2 $=$ [Number of contacts needed]

Recruitment Tabling for Contact Info

$$\frac{[\text{Contact info}]}{5 \text{ per hour}} = [\text{Person-hours}] \qquad \frac{[\text{Person-hours}]}{[\text{Total Available Hours}]} = [\text{People per hour}]$$

Class Presentations

$$\frac{[\text{Contact info}]}{.10 \text{ (percent of the class)}} = [\text{Students to speak to}] \qquad \frac{[\text{Students to speak to}]}{[\text{Average class size}]} = [\text{Number of Classes}]$$

> [ ] Denotes a number you put in or get out of the equation

Planning your Recruitment

1. **Identify your needs**: Use the outline you made when you started planning your project.

2. **Do the math**: Figure out how many contacts you need to generate based on the equations.

3. **Figure out your strategies**: Identify what blend of methods to use to get to your target

4. **Schedule it in**: Build your recruitment plan with a set timeline and factor in when you want to achieve each set of targets.

5. **Get to it**: Share your recruitment plan with your team, get feedback, and make adjustments before beginning.

Start small, grow big: Once you start your recruitment drive get your new volunteers involved immediately by plugging them into the on-going recruitment effort. If you're short on enthusiastic people to do class presentations and have an amazing new volunteer, get him/her up to speed and out doing them! Constantly challenge and engage new people they'll be excited about doing more.

Places to Recruit

- **High walking traffic areas**: Identify the main stretch of campus or a certain walking path that everyone goes through. You know your campus the best, so get out there and find those places
- **Large Classrooms**: Classes with 200-300 people can generate an average of 25 contact cards each for a few minutes of speaking so they are great places to recruit quickly and with little effort.
- **Student Union**: People around the student center are less hurried, more relaxed and more invested in the campus.
- **Outside the Library**: People going in and out of the library are there to study for extended periods of time, so talking to them is typically a welcome change of pace.

When to Recruit: Recruit when your fellow students are the least pre-occupied and have more time available. The hours around lunch are great because there are a lot of people on campus and they have at least a few moments to talk to you. The first few weeks of each quarter or semester work well. After most midterms are over and before the rush to study for finals works also.

Tabling

Tabling is the tried and true method for mobilizing your fellow students. Put a table out in a highly trafficked area of campus with a poster on display communicating the message about your cause. This involves active face to face contact with other students, engaging them in a short discussion on your issue and getting them to take action in some form or another while they are walking by. You could be getting them to volunteer for a hunger awareness event, register to vote or sign a petition to make textbooks cheaper, for example.

Tips for Tabling:

- **Be ACTIVE**: Nothing gets someone's attention like a stranger coming up and talking to them. It makes them feel important. Sitting behind a table may get you a couple interested people each hour, but engaging people face to face generates anywhere from 8-20 actions every hour, PER PERSON. Cut down the time you need to table by going out for a couple hours with a bunch of people and actively pursuing your goal.

- **The Smile and Wave**: When approaching people to talk to start about 10 feet away from the person. Make eye contact, smile and give them a small wave to get their attention.

- **Be friendly**: Present a calm and collected appearance. You might be nervous, but don't show it. You want to make people comfortable when talking to you.

- **Ask everyone**: Don't exclude people because they don't fit the "type" you're looking for – you'd be surprised just how many people will be supportive of your cause.

- **Practice**: If you're new to tabling or working on a new project, it always helps to run through the script with another person and pretend you are really doing it. This helps you identify your weak spots and build confidence in your abilities before being exposed to the real thing.

- **Shrug off rejection**: You'll talk to a lot of people who will not agree with you, give you the cold shoulder, or just plain ignore you. Don't let it get you down, because just around the corner you're going to find someone who really appreciates what you're doing.

- **Keep going**: Haven't managed to get any signatures on the petition despite being out asking people for an hour? It happens. Take a moment to review what you've been doing, practice with a friend, hone your skills and get back out there.

- **Develop your own style**: Once you become comfortable with the topic adjust the script to fit your personality. This makes your speech more genuine and will make you less nervous.

- **Remember to say thank you**: No matter what, always say thank you when parting from someone. They may have just ignored you, but at least they'll remember that you kept your cool and maybe they'll listen next time.

Student Activity Center Referenda
Pledge to Vote Card

Name: _____

Phone: _____

E-Mail: _____

Interested in Volunteering? ☐

Louisiana State University student government
http://www.sg.lsu.edu/

66

Sample Tabling Script: Textbooks Affordability

[Make eye contact, smile, and wave from 10 feet away.]

—Hi! How are you today? Do you have a minute to sign this petition urging textbooks publishers to create unbundled versions of their textbooks?

—I'm part of the Textbooks Affordability campaign in our student government and we're working on making textbooks more affordable for students. Currently textbooks are bundled with materials that the majority of professors say has little to no value to their class. So last year, in conjunction with other schools, we were able to pressure textbooks publishers into releasing the popular physics book separate from the solutions manual and study guide. This year we're trying to achieve the same thing with the biology and statistics books.

—All we need is to demonstrate student's desire to have unbundled books by sending in this petition. [Hold out clipboard and petition] Will you sign this petition? It'll only take a minute.

—Would you be interested in helping out with this campaign?

—Thank you and have a great day!

Template Tabling Script:

The Catch: Make eye contact, smile and wave from about 10 feet away.

Intro: Greet them in a comfortable way. Be confident but not too forward. Ask them for exactly what you want. If they're not at all interested they'll let you know right away.

Problem: Say who you are and what you're working on. Explain why it is important that the person you are talking to take action immediately.

Solution: Present the actions you are taking to solve the problem and why they'll work.

Explain how they can help: Reassert your request for them to take action and how little work it will be on their part.

Finish: If they seem to be interested, ask if they want to help out and give them the opportunity. Thank them for their help and wish them well.

Class Presentations

Talking in front of hundreds of your peers can be a scary and exhilarating experience. Class presentations can be the most efficient use of your time because you can reach a large group of people in a matter of minutes. The downside is that it's large, impersonal, people can easily avoid listening to you and most people hate public speaking.

Tips for Class Presentations

- **Confidence is Key**: To mobilize a classroom full of students speak with authority. If you don't you risk being ignored.

- **Practice**: Know your script, but more importantly know the material. You might accidentally skip or forget something. The audience won't know you missed something if you don't stumble.

- **Talk Loudly**: Make sure you can be heard in the back of the room and that you can get the attention of people whispering .

- **Move around**: Make hand motions, walk around the stage, make eye contact all around the audience. Be active to keep their attention.

- **Watch your posture**: Stand up straight and keep your body under control. Watch out for slouching, crossed legs, or hands behind your back, and avoid fidgeting. Look calm and confident.

- **Interact with the students**: Ask questions and force your audience to interact maybe by a show of hands. This gets them engaged in what you have to say.

- **Keep it short**: Your speech should be 2-3 minutes and never more than 5 minutes. Students' attention span is short, so get to the point as soon as possible.

Getting Clearance

Call and e-mail the professors for the classes you want to target prior to showing up at the class. They will appreciate you asking permission and you can find out when is best to come. Frequently they'll tell you one class day is better than another because of tests, important lectures, etc. Plan accordingly.

Sample Class Presentation Script: Voter Registration Drive

INTRODUCTION: Hi everyone, my name is _____ with the Voter Registration Initiative in student government. I'd like to start off by thanking Professor _____ for allowing me to speak.

PROBLEM: How many of you are registered to vote? How many of you voted in the last election? Young people ages 18-24 vote at nearly half the rate that older people do. That means that politicians don't need our votes to get elected so they don't pay attention to issues that concern young people, like the high cost of higher education, affordable textbooks prices and a future we can look forward to.

SOLUTION: Over the next month we're registering students to vote all over the school and holding events to educate all of you about the major issues of this upcoming election. Our goal is to register over 2,000 new students to vote and turn out at least a quarter of the school to the polls on Election Day!

HOW THEY CAN HELP: If you have never registered to vote, we're passing around voter registration cards which we'll collect in a few minutes when you're done. If you've recently changed addresses you should register again at your current address. Remember to fill out the form completely and accurately otherwise you won't be registered to vote. We'll keep the information private, and we'll be dropping off the forms in the next few days.

WRAP-UP: When you're done please pass the forms to the center aisle and I will collect them in the next few minutes. Thank you again for your attention and thanks professor _____. Have a great day!

Template Class Presentation Script:

Introduction: Who you are, what organization you're from. Remember to thank the professor!

Problem: Use your project's message to highlight important facts, statistics and stories.

Solution: Present the actions you are taking to solve the problem and why they'll work.

How they can help: Be direct and tell the audience what they need to do to help, whether it is filling out a voter registration form or writing their contact info down.

Wrap-Up: Explain how you are going to collect the materials (give explicit instructions). Thank the audience and the professor again. Collect your things and go.

Contact Calling

This tool is one of the best methods for making sure things are going to happen. Getting confirmations for attendance, reminding someone that they signed up for an activity, or calling someone for the first time to get them involved can all be done very quickly and easily over the phone.

Tips for Contact Calling:

- **Be confident**: You'll frequently be calling someone while they are in the middle of doing something so be quick and polite. They did want you to call by filling out a contact form so don't feel like you're intruding.

- **Always confirm**: Many people will shy away from committing to a specific time, but be diligent in asking what time they can volunteer for. Don't count unconfirmed people in any totals because you can't guarantee that they'll show up since they didn't set a time.

- **Give alternatives**: Many people want to get involved but will not be able to make it to your primary activity, so give them alternative events where they can get connected.

- **Avoid leaving messages**: Do a second round of calling on a different day to try to talk to them on the phone. People will not usually call back. Leaving a message closes the avenues to contact. You don't want to seem too aggressive by calling them again when they haven't even returned the first message.

- **Be prepared for callbacks**: Some people will call back later or the next day. Be prepared to explain what you were calling about and be able to answer questions without the script in front of you.

Sample Calling Script: Beginning of the Year Student Government Recruitment

Hi, can I speak with _____?

Hello, this is _____ with Missouri State University Student Government. How are you?

Good. I am calling because you filled out a contact card saying you were interested in getting involved in student government. I just wanted to let you know that we're having an information session on Tuesday, September 30th at 7pm in the student government offices. Do you think you can make this?

[If yes, then mark off on attendance sheet.]

We're also having a tabling event outside of Strong Hall from 11am to 2pm the following day to rally support against student financial aid cuts by getting students to sign petition postcards to send in to the governor. We'll be training people to help on the spot so don't worry if you haven't done this before. Can you help with this?

[If yes or maybe continue, otherwise skip to the end]

Which hour could you make it? We really want to make sure we have people committed to every time slot so we know what to expect.

Great! Thank you so much. We'll see you at _____ (date, time confirmed and location). Bye!

Online Organizing

Online communication and social networking websites provide a nearly endless array of possibilities for mobilizing your peers. They also come with drawbacks because of the sheer amount of content available. Don't solely use on-line strategies to achieve your goals. Make use of these methods as part of an overall plan incorporating both on-line and off-line mechanisms.

E-Mail:

- **Positives**: E-mail provides a quick and easy way to get information to fellow students. It generates a limited amount of action but requires very little time on your part.

- **Negatives**: Your e-mail will get deleted or ignored because of its inability to motivate action. You also have to compete with all the other e-mails being sent out.

- **How to use it to your advantage**: E-mail is mainly used to inform your target group. Keep it short and focused on the few priority events or issues. You can always give them a link to more information and actions they could take on a website if they're really interested. You can also use it to conduct unbiased surveys if you send it out to enough people.

> **Warning**: On-line mechanisms are not substitutes to real, on the ground actions. They can be used to supplement the overall plan but not relied upon to generate success. On-line activities are too variable to count on them to help you succeed. They are too prone to overuse. Your audience will tune out.

Social Networking Sites:

- **Positives**: Groups, causes and event tools combined with widespread use among university students.

- **Negatives**: No guarantee that your efforts at mobilization will create action despite wide use by students.

- ### How to use it to your advantage

    a. Social networking sites are great for viral or word of mouth mobilization. Allow enough time for this to work. Use the groups to have your friends invite their friends and have their friends invite more friends for all sorts of common interest groups. You can then use this group to disseminate information or attempt to mobilize them for an event.

    b. When preparing for an event, create an event invitation far enough in advance so that a reasonable amount of people can see the event is taking place. This also helps to get a good minimum estimate of attendance.

    c. Groups can also help to bring together students around a central and clearly defined cause. There are also many functions like donations, announcements, and recruitment that make a good choice for mobilizing around issues.

Instant Messaging:

- **Positives**: You can disseminate information quickly through people's social networks, especially when it calls for immediate action, like reminding people to vote on Election Day.

- **Negatives**: You can never tell how far the message will penetrate or whether people will be willing to participate by passing it along.

- **How to use it to your advantage**: Make a very short message – one sentence or a link. Make it matter. Make sure this is a message you would be willing to send out to your buddy list.

Retention

You can't forget about all the people that make your campaigns or events so successful day after day. Most people who get involved in student government genuinely care about making the campus a better and more exciting place. That doesn't mean that their passion is inexhaustible or that they'll stay around if they are treated poorly. This is why retaining your commissioners, interns or volunteers is so important. They represent the compilation of experience and knowledge that drives your successful projects day in and day out.

Suggestions for Retention:

- **Be real**: Nothing spoils the mood like fake appreciation. Be authentically invested in your co-workers and show interest in their lives.

- **Be honest**: If there are problems with the event or project try to figure out a way to incorporate everyone into fixing it. Make it a team effort rather than an individual call.

- **Build a relationship**: Get to know each other outside of the student government work environment. Arrange for your team to grab something to eat after long work sessions or plan a department outing. Some of the best and most effective projects are done by people who love to work together and have fun together.

- **Make work fun**: People will do an amazing amount of work without any kind of reward except their own gratification, but if you can throw a little fun into a draining task it can boost motivation.

Summary

Mobilizing the student body is one of the most time and energy intensive activities student governments engage in. Person to person or grassroots organizing relies on a great deal of planning and identifying important target numbers to reach in order to achieve success. One of the first parts of student mobilization is recruitment of students into the project group so you'll have enough people to engage students on your campus. This is normally achieved through one of the primary mobilizing strategies. Once you've identified the needs for your project, there are number of strategies to use to achieve your goal: getting a table out on the main stretch of campus, speaking to large classrooms before class starts, calling people interested or committed to the cause, and mobilizing students on-line. The right combination of strategies will help you achieve success with your project, and allow both you and your group to be rewarded for their achievement.

Chapter 7: Planning - The Key to Winning

Planning is an outline of your project, starting with establishing your goals and going through every step you need to take to accomplish those goals. To win you have to be willing to achieve all the incremental steps along the way. If you try to do all aspects of the project without planning, your lofty ideas will fall flat on their face. Planning is the most important part of initiating any campaign. It makes every part of the project come together in an organized and orderly way.

Planning takes into account nearly every skill and concept covered in this manual. If you haven't spent a few minutes reviewing the general concepts do that now so you know what to put in the plan. Take the time on the front end of your project to put together a good, well thought out plan. This will save you from a lot of stress and wasted effort later in the project.

Beware: All too often people will wait until the last minute and try to get everything done at once. Avoid the stress and the frantic last minute mess by putting in the work on the front end to figure out what things need to get done and when. This ensures you don't forget something important.

Saving Your Precious Time by Spending Time Planning

The more prepared and organized you are the more time you'll save by not wasting it on the activities you'd rather not be doing. It seems counterintuitive that the extra task of planning out your week, month, or semester would give you more time. It will keep you on track for your goals and avoid the unimportant and ineffective tasks.

Work Backwards

Once you've determined when you want to achieve victory or hold your event its time to think about how and when you need to execute each of your strategies. Start from the day of the event or campaign victory and think back through each day and week leading up to the event. Determine what things need to happen and in which order so that will result in achieving your goal or reaching the next step of your plan. There is no quick way to do this step because you must think back through every step you will need to take. This involves working through one strategy all the way to the beginning and may require you to utilize multiple different strategies in order to achieve your final targets.

For example, let's say your publicity target is to hang 400 posters the week before an event. After thinking about the actual mechanics of putting up the posters, you determine that to get them put up you need to have the posters printed and a team of people confirmed to put them up on a specific day. You'll need to do those things the week before. To get to the week 3 actions you'll need to have the poster design sent out to get printed, but you'll also need to recruit people this week so you'll have everything set the following week. Finally, the week before this you need to design the poster and get it approved.

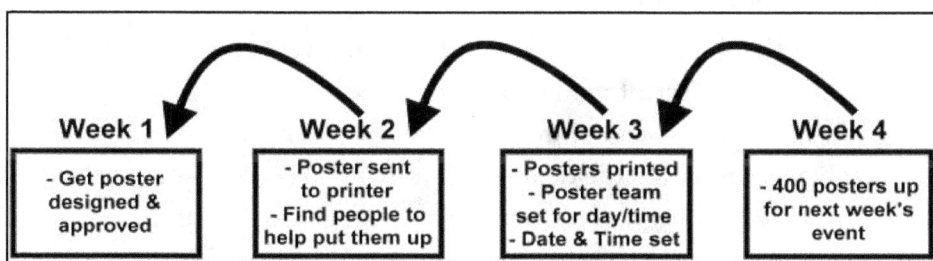

Week 1	Week 2	Week 3	Week 4
- Get poster designed & approved	- Poster sent to printer - Find people to help put them up	- Posters printed - Poster team set for day/time - Date & Time set	- 400 posters up for next week's event

Working backwards helps you make sure you plan for all the details that each task will require by evaluating what you need to do to get to each successive step. Make sure you accomplish all the tasks early enough to be able to stick to the timeline and accomplish your goal on time.

Make a Weekly Action Plan

Doing weekly plans is one of the underappreciated gems of planning that allows you to spend your time wisely. Get a planner to help you keep on top of the tasks you decide you need to do each day. Get into the habit of doing this and you will have more free time and a lot less stress. Take your plans for this week from your long term plan and figure out what you need to do each day and how much time you think it will take. (See Template Weekly Action Plan in this chapter)

- **Pick out your primary priorities for the week**: Keep your list of priorities around two or three. Keep your attention focused on completing the most important tasks rather than getting bogged down in unimportant and ineffective tasks (See Setting Priorities and Time Management)

> ### Stressed and Don't have Enough Time to do a Weekly Plan? Think Again!
>
> How much time to do spend every week on time wasting activities? Probably more than the hour it takes to plan your week, doing something you don't want to or have to do. Instead, put that time to good use by planning out the week ahead and you'll find you have even more time to do what you really want to do.

- **Fill in the target objectives you want to accomplish**: This could be your recruitment goals for your upcoming event, people you need to meet with or even a big essay you need to devote time to. By writing down the details and numerical goals you'll be able to measure your progress towards getting everything done.

- **Break Targets down by day**: Write down each activity that needs to get done and how much time you think it would take next to each day of the week. Set specific time limits on all tasks in your planner. (See Time Management for methods on scheduling time)

> **Note**: To make the best use of your weekly plan consider including other responsibilities like homework or other clubs you are involved in so you have a truly accurate and personalized schedule.

- **Set daily priorities:** Figure out what tasks absolutely need to get done each day. These should be the first tasks you work on each day because there will be distractions that come up throughout the day that will take away from your available time.

- **Leave space for free time:** This will prevent you from over-working yourself to the point of exhaustion. Just because you can save time by doing things more effectively it doesn't mean you should fill it with more work. Leaving some time will give you some leeway when new things come up or projects take longer.

- **Put a limit on the work you do:** More work is not necessarily better work. Give yourself a chance to do a really good job on a couple of activities rather than spreading yourself across too many

Weekly Action Plan

Name: <u>Alexis Madison</u>
Position: <u>Textbooks Director</u>
Week: <u>January 21st — 27th</u>

Major Priorities:
1.) <u>Meet w/ the Bookstore Director</u>
2.) <u>Write textbooks survey</u>
3.) <u>Train new intern</u>

Priorities	Objectives and Targets	Check-Off
Priority #1: Meet with the Bookstore Director	Have a meeting to determine viability and next steps for the 5 year guarantee	
Priority #2: Write textbooks survey	Complete writing 10 question survey and send to Martin for review	
Priority #3: Train new intern	Prepare handout and brief leadership training for new intern Jimmy	X
Schoolwork:	Read 40 pages for history Tuesday, 6-8 page essay in Soc. due Thursday	X
Other Responsibilities:	Community Service Club meeting Thursday night, prepare fun activity	
People to meet with:	Meet with Jimmy to determine his areas of interest and plug him into the project	X
Prep Work for Next Week:	Write out implementation strategy for survey. E-mail interns to find out the best time for the survey training.	

Day by Day Outline:

Monday: Write survey (10am-12pm)
Read for history (1-2pm, 8-10pm)
Tuesday: Training handout (2-3pm)
Work on essay (6-9pm)
Wednesday: Meet with Jimmy (3-4pm)
Prep for club meeting (4-5pm)
Work on essay (8-11pm)
Thursday: Prep for meeting (6-7pm)
Club Meeting (7-8:30pm)

Friday: Bookstore meeting (9-10am)
Send survey to Martin (10-10:30am)
Saturday: E-mail interns (1-1:30pm)
Sunday: Implementation strategy (2-4pm)

Total Student Government Hours: 9 hours

Steps to Effective Planning

Planning is a long and involved process to outline your path to success. Throughout these steps we'll use an example to help you absorb the concepts at each step. Let's start with the premise that your campus is now at 16,000 students which means it is quickly out-growing its event facilities and it needs a new center for concerts, sports and large scale events.

- **Brainstorming**: Before you start putting down any specifics goals and objectives take some time to mull over the problem you want to address. Get excited – think about different aspects of the problem, and creative ways to solve it.

- **Find your Vision**: The over-all objective you want to achieve. Make it as broad as necessary to encompass your vision.

- **Establish your Goals**: Using your vision, determine a specific objective you want to accomplish. What would you consider an accomplishment or a victory?

Campus Events Center Campaign Planning:

-- Brainstorming: The largest room for events on campus only fits 600 people and we've wanted to put on a large concert for a larger portion of the campus. Graduation and other events are also out-growing this venue.

-- Vision: We want to put on amazing new events for a large portion of the student body.

-- Goals: Build a new events center to accommodate the growing needs of the campus by getting the student body to vote to increase their tuition by a set amount of money to help fund the construction.

- **Select Appropriate Strategies**: Strategies are methods you use to achieve your goal such as using "visibility" for putting up posters or "recruitment" when you need to get more people involved. The specifics of these strategies are in Chapter 6. Skim them to know what you have at your disposal.

-- Strategies

Visibility: Posters, Fliers, T-Shirts, Online, Website, News Ads

Recruitment: Tabling, Class presentations, Calling

Media: Local papers, campus paper, campus radio

Mobilization: Tabling, Calling

Coalition Building: Campus Administration, Faculty, Clubs and Or-

- **Set your Targets**: Targets should be a specific number you are shooting for that will be sufficient to achieve your goals. Your targets should *never* be arbitrary, but represent an educated guess at what you think you need to achieve success. More is not always better. Keep what you consider a victory in mind and what you honestly think it will take to get you there. In this section you will calculate the intermediate goals you need to hit in order to achieve your objectives using the discounting rule. (See Student Mobilization)

-- Targets

Goal Target: A simple majority vote is required by the student body, and at least 25% of the student body must vote in the election in order for the referendum to qualify according to the university rules. So we need to get a minimum of **4,000 students** out to vote (16,000 x .25 = 4,000) and at least **2,000 to vote yes** (4,000 x .50 = 2,000). To give us a comfortable enough margin we should shoot for **4,500 total votes** (500 vote margin) and at least **2,750 yes votes** (500 vote margin on 50% of the new vote total). On the day of campus elections we need to be confident that are going to reach our target number, so we will use the discounting rule to figure out how to get there.

Voter Mobilization: Because the total votes and yes votes are tied together we decide to influence and record committed yes votes during the general voter mobilization. We decide we are going to get half of the direct commitments, and phone numbers so we can confirm later, from tabling and use other strategies to mobilize the rest. The **2,250 from tabling** can be calculated using the following: your team can get about 15 confirmed contacts per hour, so that is 150 person-hours of tabling which, if we plan on tabling for 4 hours each day, the two weeks leading up to the election (4 hrs/day x 5 days/week x 2 weeks = 40 hrs), we need about **4 people every hour**.

Because people occasionally cannot make it we will schedule **300 person-hours**, twice as many as we need. We decide that each person who is on the team will be really committed and will agree to do an average of 20 hours over the two weeks of campaigning. This means that we need to **recruit 15 people** for the team for tabling (300 person-hrs/20 hrs per person=15 people). We decide we can get most of those people from within student government, and a few more during the initial week of campaigning.

This part of the example only covered one of the strategies from step #4 and you can already see how complicated but important this planning step is. Take a look at the sample plan for a more detailed diagram of the entire campaign.

- **Create a Timetable**: Figure out when you want to accomplish your goal and successfully execute each of your strategies. Set it at a reasonable and appropriate time in the future. Concerts can rarely be put together in a week, and a media generating event works best when it coincides with the major event you are trying to affect. One strategy will need to be completed before another can commence. To determine how and when to reach each of your targets use the backwards planning model which we've already practiced while doing targeting estimates.

-- **Timetable:** We need to have 15 team members ready to go two weeks from the election day. To get there we need to have everyone trained the week before. To get people to the training we need to have a date, time, and location set the week before that. We also need to have our team members set the week before the training so we can get them there, which means the week prior if not two weeks before we need to send out an announcement to the entire student government to get people to volunteer, as well as asking around and recruiting people.

Planning Events

Putting on large and small scale events is one of the most common activities that student governments do. Planning for these events follows the same practices as any other type of project, with a couple of special notes. As part of your planning for the quarter/semester or year you should always include the events you plan on doing. This section will provide a few tips for specifically planning events.

- **Think Ahead**: Starting the planning process early will add to a great event idea. Many events suffer from a lack of planning, and especially planning early enough to get everything done. Don't put off planning and throw something together at the last minute.

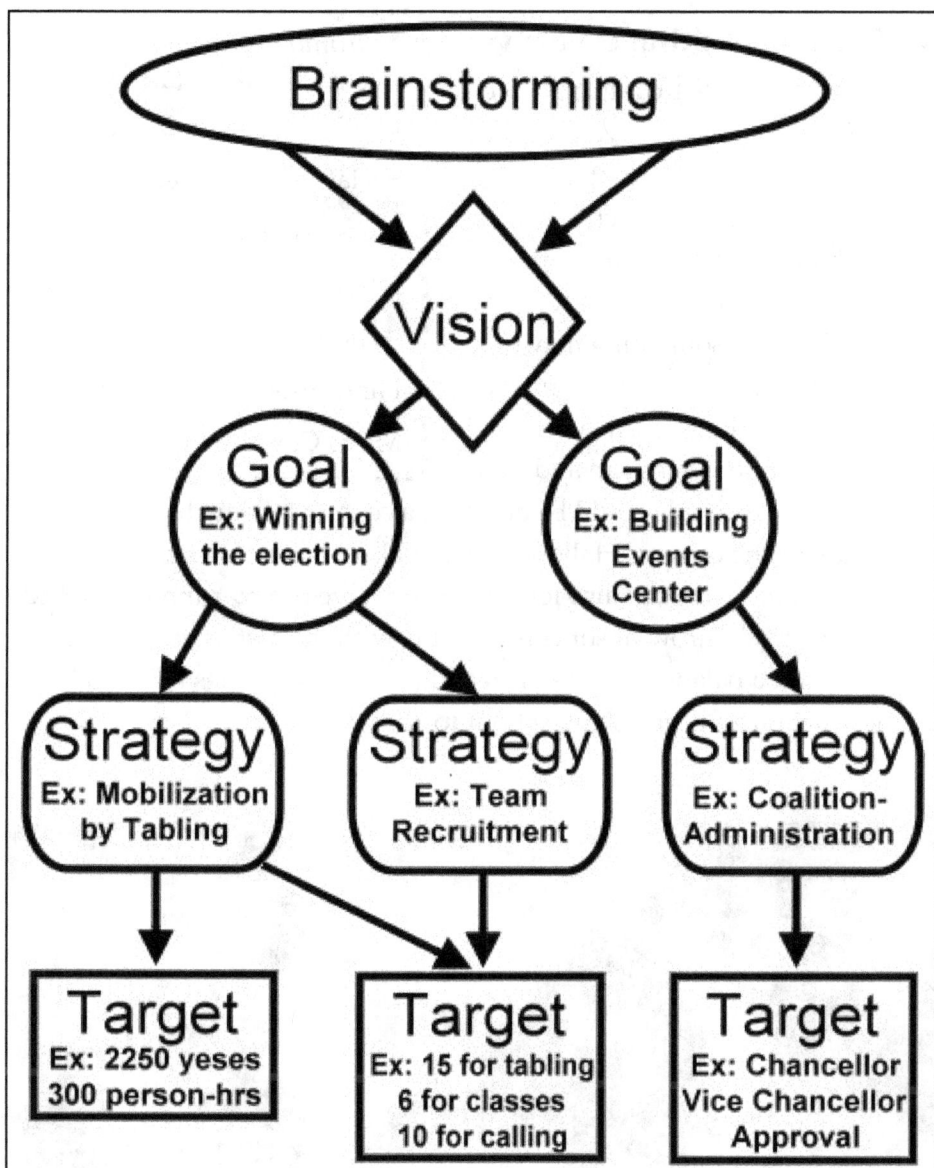

Brainstorming → Vision → Goal / Goal → Strategy / Strategy / Strategy → Target / Target / Target

Vision

Goal — Ex: Winning the election

Goal — Ex: Building Events Center

Strategy — Ex: Mobilization by Tabling

Strategy — Ex: Team Recruitment

Strategy — Ex: Coalition-Administration

Target — Ex: 2250 yeses, 300 person-hrs

Target — Ex: 15 for tabling, 6 for classes, 10 for calling

Target — Ex: Chancellor Vice Chancellor Approval

- **Details, Details, Details:** Events often require many more details to be completed to make it amazing. This is why procrastination and poor preparation are the blight of event planning. Be sure to write down everything you need to get done, down to every detail. This practice will pay off in the long run with less stress and a better event.

86

- **Fun and exciting events vs. effective but boring**: All work and no play may get you to your goals this time, but that may be as far as you get. As much as we like to think of ourselves and others as work machines it just isn't the case. Just because something may seem less effective, doesn't mean you won't get a boost from an intangible result known as fun and excite-

Minimum Recommended
Event Planning start time:

Petition/Tabling: 2 weeks

Social/Fun: 2-3 weeks

Press/Media: 3 weeks

Entertainment: 1-2 months

Action/Protest: 2-3 months

Fundraisers: 2-3 months

Major Concerts: 4-6 months

ment. An example could be building a costume themed after your issue for the campus Halloween festival. This generates a buzz around the issue but also lets the group have fun by running around the festival. Throw in some fun events with the rest of your schedule. Find a balance between fun and practical activities that still lets you achieve the goals you set out to accomplish.

GOALS	WEEK 0	WEEK 1	WEEK 2	WEEK 3	WEEK 4	WEEK 5	WEEK 6	WEEK 7	WEEK 8	WEEK 9	WEEK 10	VOTING WEEK	WEEK 12
FACULTY/ADMINISTRATION ~Chancellor approval ~Planning department on board ~Ensure passage through Administration after vote	~Research Administrators who deal with campus planning and decision making	~Invite selected administrators to a meeting	~Meet with administrators to work out technical details, needs and space	~Meet with campus planning to review money needs		~2nd meeting with administrators to go over referenda draft	~Schedule meeting with Chancellor to discuss later approval and present final draft						~Passage through Administrative Approval process
CLUBS & ORGS ~Endorsement from 100 clubs ~Form coalition with 15 largest organizations						~Compile club lists with contact information	~Contact club leaders to schedule time to go to club meetings	~Meet with 50 clubs ~20 endorsements ~5 new coalition members	~Meet with 50 clubs ~35 endorsements ~5 new coalition members	~Meet with 50 clubs ~45 endorsements ~5 new coalition members		~Clubs inform their members to vote for the referendum	
VISIBILITY ~2000 Campaign posters up ~12000 Fliers passed out ~50 T-shirts ~1 major visibility event				~Craft message for campaign ~Brainstorm visual ideas	~Design publicity materials (posters, fliers, t-shirts)	~Send designs out for printing		~Receive all major supplies	~Prep for visibility event	~Visibility event ~2000 fliers passed out ~500 campaign posters up ~T-shirts distributed to mobilization teams	~4000 fliers passed out ~500 campaign posters up	~6000 fliers passed out ~1000 campaign posters up	
ONLINE ~1000 people in campaign group ~E-mails sent out to committed voters						~Build campaign website	~Create on-line group		~Online invitations and recruitment		~Send out update & info about referenda	~E-mail all confirmed voters	
RECRUITMENT ~15 for tabling ~6 for class presentations ~10 for contact calling		~E-mail/contact student government members	~10 recruited from student government					~5 people recruited from clubs	~5 people recruited from clubs	~5 people recruited from clubs ~6 people recruited from class presentations			
NEWS MEDIA ~3 positive news articles in campus paper ~5 Letters to the Editor ~1 positive editorial								~Meet with campus newspaper reporters to pitch the new Events Center referenda	~1 positive article about introduction of new referenda	~Meet with Editor in Chief of campus newspaper to discuss editorial	~1 positive article on rally event ~5 letters to the editor	~1 positive news article ~1 positive editorial	
MOBILIZATION ~2350 yeses from tabling (300 hrs) ~250 yeses from class presentations (75 classes) ~4500 called before election								~Prepare training materials	~Tabling & class presentation training	~1250 yeses from tabling (150 hrs) ~1250 yeses from class presentations (35 classes) ~Tabling & class presentation training	~1000 yeses from tabling (150 hrs) ~1000 yeses from class presentations (40 classes) ~Tabling & class presentation training ~Calling training	~Remind people to vote tabling ~Class presentations to remind people to vote ~900 calls per day to confirmed voters (4500 total calls)	
TECHNICAL/LOGISTICS ~Referenda written ~Monetary plans for events center set	~Research path and requirements for referenda passage		~Begin writing referenda language ~Begin monetary calculations for the new Events Center	~1st draft of referenda written	~2nd draft written	~Referenda written	~Revise and submit to Student Senate for review and vote	~Submit referenda to elections board				~Voting takes place	~Referenda moves to administration for approval

How to Use Your Plan

- **Re-evaluate your plan at least once a week:** Figure out if you've kept up with the goals and timeline. If not, try to determine why you're off track.

- **Adjust your plan as needed:** If you're off track figure out what you have to do to still hit your goals. If necessary, adjust your goal up or down if it's no longer realistic. Add new projects and events that come up during the quarter. Don't feel boxed in to the original plan. Take advantage of new opportunities that present themselves.

- **Choose your weekly priorities based on your plan:** What are the most important things to focus on this week? Today? Pick things that absolutely have to get done. Stay on track by having a clear vision of what needs to be done.

- **Use your plan to figure out what you realistically can expect to get done:** Everything that you cannot get done by yourself delegate to others. Use the plan to delegate tasks ahead of time and help ensure that more is going on than only what you have time to do.

Avoiding Planning Pitfalls

- **Don't dishearten if your plan isn't working**: Don't stop using your plan if doesn't work exactly as you had planned. Plans look very different by the time you are done. Things are always changing. Take time to re-evaluate the original plan and strategize new solutions. You may be on the right track, but just need a few tweaks.

- **Plans only work if you follow them**: If you write the plan and then don't look at it again it is useless. Once you've put all the work into your plan follow through on your goals.

- **Avoiding planning will put off your goals**: Sometimes things work out without any planning at all. Most of the time it will not work that way, or at least not the way you want. If you want to achieve your goals: plan, plan early, and plan often.

- **Stay away from overall goals that are vague or un-achievable**: You want to know what you're working towards and know when you've succeeded. Shooting for a realistically ambitious goal is much more likely to succeed than setting your weight against gigantic problems. World peace is a great goal but its going to require a much, much longer plan.

- **Mind your surroundings and do your research**: Know the status and situation of your issue. Know who else is passionate about it and who opposes it. The more you know the better you'll be able to custom tailor your plan to achieve victory. Make the plan fit reality and you'll achieve it!

Summary:

Planning your project relies on skills covered in every chapter of this manual and integrates all the strategies you decide you need to use. Planning before you start your project will save you far more time and energy during execution. Working backwards allows you to identify the intermediate targets you need to hit in order to hit your overall targets later. The steps to planning allow you to build the scale and objectives of your project in a methodical way so that all of your goals come from realistic targets. You can also use the Weekly Action Plan to break down your plan ever farther to identify your most important objectives to accomplish each week.

Glossary

Class Presentation: Giving a short 2-3 minute speech in a classroom full of students in order to mobilize them into action, informing them about some important news, and find the people interested in volunteering. This strategy is effective in generating contact information from pledges or interest in a certain issue which can be used to follow up when the date of an event or action is coming up.

Coalition Building: Forming an organization out of a number of separate groups interested in accomplishing the same goal. This allows different parts of the coalition to focus on their strengths and pool their resources for the benefit of the cause or project.

Contact Calling: Is a method for getting confirmations and identifying people interested in a particular campaign or project. Contact information is typically collected from tabling or class presentations. Calling ensures that individuals get connected into the project or reminded about an event.

Discounting Rule: When planning your project you use the discounting rule to estimate the numerical intermediate goals that you need to hit in order to reach your overall goal.

Goals: With regard to planning, your goals are the tangible results you want to have at the end of your project.

Messaging: Is the way of phrasing statements connected with your project in order to communicate with your target groups in the most effective way possible.

Parliamentary Procedure: The rules that guide official decision making in groups that have adopted these guidelines. They allow equal debate and decision making in a group.

Postering: This involves putting up posters and other advertising material up around your campus in order to publicize an event or project.

Power Mapping: A way of charting out the power structure of important decision makers and potential allies that have influence over achieving the goal of your project.

Press Advisory: This is an invitation for an event that is sent to members of the press to let them know what is going on and invite them to come and report on the activity.

Press Release: A complete article written as the ideal story that is reported. It is send to the press with all the information they need to write an article of their own.

Recruitment: A term for getting students involved in a project that needs additional help and more people to get the goals accomplished.

Retention: A method for keeping volunteers and leaders involved in the project or organization.

Strategy: A method or type of action used in accomplishing a goal for a project.

Table/Tabling: Tabling is a strategy for mobilizing the student body. Students will put out a table with informational materials and frequently an eye catching banner or visual to draw other students' attention. The main goal of the table is to generate action by actively approaching students in a friendly way while they walk by in order to ask them to help take action or inform them about an important issue that affects them.

Target: Specific numerical or tangible results that you need to accomplish using the strategies chosen for your project.

Vision: The aspirational objective you are trying to achieve with your project. This should be a general and inspiring statement of what you are trying to achieve.

Weekly Action Plan: A plan for your week, taking objectives from your long term plan and fitting them into your schedule so that you can accomplish them in an orderly way.

www.ingramcontent.com/pod-product-compliance
Lightning Source LLC
Chambersburg PA
CBHW070256290326
41930CB00041B/2596